Better By The Dozen Plus Two, Part Two:

Lessons Learned through Loss and Leukemia by a Family of Sixteen

Better By The Dozen Plus Two, Part Two:

Lessons Learned through Loss and Leukemia by a Family of Sixteen

By Kathleen Littleton

**Praise for the author's first book *Better By the Dozen Plus Two,*
subtitled *Anecdotes and a Philosophy Of Life From A Family of
Sixteen* co-authored with James Littleton**

"Here's a family you won't forget. And reading about them will
brighten your day and deepen your faith. I was blessed in meeting
them because their three oldest girls attended or attend Ave Maria
University—and we're hoping the 11 younger siblings will follow
in their footsteps! You'll find 16 reasons for being joyfully
counter-cultural."
Fr. Joseph D. Fessio, S.J.
Editor, Ignatius Press and Theologian in Residence, Ave Maria
University

"In Better by the Dozen, Plus Two James and Kathleen Littleton
have written a truly profound book that may change your family
forever. Through Scripture, Catechism, family anecdotes, and
simple 'how to' practical advice, this work will challenge and
inspire all families both large and small. Throughout the book one
thing is clear; the Littleton family perseveres and thrives because
of God's Sacramental Grace. Read this book and be encouraged.
Read this book and be awed. Read this book and learn how you,
too, can raise a family firmly rooted in Faith and Love for Christ
and His Church."
Mark and Elizabeth Matthews
Authors of *Precious Treasure, The Story of Patrick* and *A Place
for Me*

"For those looking to invite God not just to their wedding, but also
into their marriage, this is a must read. The Littleton's personal
journey in striving to be open to God's will, and then to live his
will, offers the inspiration and tools to accomplish this in our own
lives."
Kris Cortes
Co-founder, *Virtue in Action* and *Our Faith in Action*

From Amazon.com:

"Superb! Superb! Superb! I read this book at least once a year. I am now in my fourth reading since purchasing it. You will fall in love with this large, Irish Catholic family, as I have. Jim and Kathleen Littleton are devout Catholics who have not been afraid to make radical choices when it comes to living a Christ-centered life or raising a family in such a way that goes completely against the grain of the dominant culture. They have been such an inspiration to me. In fact, after my husband read this book, he decided to become a Catholic! The Littletons have 14 living children. In this book, they will share with you what they are convinced are God's Hierarchy of Values, namely, God, Spouse, Children, Work, and then Service Work/Apostolate. They also discuss Marriage, Motherhood, Openness to Life, Formation of Children, Service, Cross-Carrying, and the necessity of possessing a sense of humor. Whenever I become discouraged as a parent, I know that it's time to take this book off of the shelf and read it again. It is the only Catholic book on parenting and devotion that I continue to read over and over again. I eagerly await their next book, and hope that one day, there will be one.
5.0 out of 5 stars Superb! Superb! Superb!
By T.A.

"Jim and Kathleen are a beautiful example of understanding, living, and teaching the Catholic faith. I felt like I wanted to be adopted by them!"
5.0 out of 5 stars Motivating, October 12, 2007
By S.E.

"This book is proof that current cultural wisdom is wrong and that the Catholic teaching on openness to life is right. Who knows better, you or God? The Littletons are an excellent example of the generosity God is asking for. One important lesson pointed out by James and Kathleen Littleton is that the world looks at children as a burden which actually belittles the contribution that children bring. They are not just empty stomachs and brains demanding to be fed and sent to college. They are persons who contribute to the family from the day they are brought into it - and more and more as they mature.

This book was like a pleasant stroll through a different world in which values were properly prioritized. I only wish there were more anecdotes about the children's interaction with each other and the hostile world. I loved the one about two older kids saving 10 seats in a theater during the previews while the younger ones waited in the lobby so they didn't have to look at all the junk in the previews.

A good gift for your teenaged sons and daughters. A mandatory gift for Pre-Cana classes. Good idea for Engaged- and Marriage Encounter Weekend attendees."
Five Stars Countercultural May 21, 2012
By J.K.

Praise after appearance on EWTN promoting first book *Better By the Dozen Plus Two*, subtitled *Anecdotes and a Philosophy Of Life From A Family of Sixteen* co-authored with James Littleton

"Your gorgeous children and your 'radical' 'pouring out' of yourselves in your 'YES' to God amount to some of the most inspiring Faith I think I've ever seen. I was particularly moved by your profound grasp of the Faith and your easy, articulate expression of it throughout. Thank you, thank you for your gracious, generous, love-filled witness! May God continue to bless you both, and all your children, with His ever-deepening love and strength." P.B.

"Very impressive. I wish I could start over on my kids and follow their way of doing things." C.F.

"What a witness to the power and love of God and God's love for family life." B.S.

"It does my heart so much good to see that there are in the world happy families, happy marriages, Catholic lifestyle. Thank you for being a ray of sunshine in a dark, lonely world. Thank you for being open and supportive of life. I rejoice seeing happiness, seeing the right way to live, seeing Catholicism in action. Thank you for the sacrifices. Thank you for a wonderful example you are to the Mystical Body of Christ, to the world." V.M.

"Talk about a domestic church! Yours is like a cathedral!" S.S.

Dedication Page

This book was commenced on May 31, 2012, the Feast of the Assumption and was completed on August 6, 2012, the Feast of the Transfiguration.

May God do with me as He will.

I dedicate this book to my dear husband of twenty-nine years, Jim, and to my beautiful children, Shannon, Tara, Grace, Colleen, Deirdre, Bridget, Shane, Fiona, Maura, Clare, Patrick, Mairead, Brighde and Shealagh.

Without them, I am nothing.

Table of Contents

Prologue

Since we started telling our story, some readers of our first book, *Better By The Dozen Plus Two, Anecdotes and a Philosophy of Life From a Family of Sixteen,* who were helped, inspired or just plain curious, have been asking what has happened to us and our children since that writing in 2006.

I especially write this for my fourteen children so they can know what God has done, how He loves us and arranges our lives, how He is always with us, never abandoning us. May we all remember what we have learned along the way.

The ongoing story of what God has done in our lives over the past six years is a much more dramatic tale than what was told in our first book which chronicled the first twenty-three years of our married life. If the story of how God's grace can transform a contracepting, materialistic, menu-picking Catholic couple into a counter-cultural, authentically Catholic family with fourteen children may seem almost impossible, the story of what God has done since 2006 may seem quite incredible. But why should we be surprised? Is it not true that God is always with us, looking out for us, loving us, providing for us, even when we aren't aware or care?

This is a tale of what God can do, and how God loves. It is a Job story, a story of how God giveth and God taketh away, but always about how blessed is the name of the Lord.[1]

The Back of the Bottom Pantry Shelf

It was the winter of 2006 and our youngest daughter, Shealagh, was born into a family of thirteen older siblings, living in a home that was about to be foreclosed on. She and her next oldest sibling, Brighde, just barely a one-year-old, had no idea what instability surrounded them as they babbled and crawled and were held and loved profusely by everyone in the home around them.

Their devoted father had done all he could do for who could have known that when we purchased the home just three years prior after living in it for only one year we would be putting it up for sale? And who could have known that their hard-working father's established twelve-year-old business would decline and that even the second job he took on would soon come to an end due to economic budget cutting reasons? And who could have known that the home would be up for sale for two and one-half-years and never have had a single offer of purchase made upon it? And who could have known that our country was on the verge of the worst economic recession since the great depression and the booming housing market bubble was about to burst? We were one of the first victims.

We stopped buying ice cream. This indeed was a tragedy, for all the Littletons love it and find it a soothing treat on a nightly basis. But sacrifices had to be made. Other staples of the home soon too were no longer purchased as funds were in so short supply. The pantry was literally quite bare, and dinner would often consist of noodles and peanut butter and whatever canned goods might not yet be expired from the back of the bottom pantry shelf.

The home and neighborhood we lived in was quite lovely and since we could not afford lawn care or a cleaning lady but needed to maintain the external appearance of a well-cared for home, soon me and the children were out there pulling weeds and scurrying to tidy the home for the always inconveniently timed and never productive house showings. I would pile the lot of them into the impossible-to-hide stark white fifteen passenger van and drive half a block down to the neighborhood park where they played and I watched the arrival and departure of the many realtors and wishful potential buyers from a hopefully safe distance. There were times when we had a house showing at night or in bad weather when we didn't leave the house, but instead we all went down into the basement to get out of the way, only to have the house tour continue down there where we were discovered, and they discovered that yes indeed, these were all our children and yes they all did inhabit this home – perhaps not a great selling point.

Were we wrong to be open to life? Were we wrong to believe that God would provide, since He created us He would sustain us? What mistakes had we made along the way that we were now paying for? Was our faith too strong? Were we being presumptuous? And what of those other families who looked to us as an example of Catholic living? Were we failing them by our apparent failures? No. Time would reveal the truth. We were being purified, and God was stripping us of our earthly attachments so that we might come to love Him even more, rely on Him more fully and render all the glory of His saving power back to Him in testimony.

The Prophecy of a Stranger in a Dream House

By November of 2007 our time had run out. Not making our monthly mortgage payments had taken its inevitable ultimate consequence. When the doorbell rang one day and I, the attorney-at-law turned full-time-mother-of-fourteen, was served with my first summons of foreclosure proceedings, I was internally scandalized. However, the sick always anxious feeling of fearing the inevitable was worse than the anti-climatic finality.

One day we just left the house.

That day was a long time in coming. We had lived there for four years, the first year being one of ignorant-of-events-to-come bliss. The coming of the last day took a total of three years of endured house showings, four pregnancies which included two miscarriages and then beautiful Brighde and Shealagh, a month's worth of packing and giving possessions away, a year's worth of looking for a new place to live, and an unknown toll on the limits of our faith, endurance, and sanity. We just kept praying through it, relying on God and on each other for consolation and support and being consoled by the compassion and empathy of some close friends. I called it "living in the cloud of unknowing". [2]

Our plan and hope was to move back to Frankfort, the town in which we had lived since 1988, where nine of our children had been born and our first twelve had lived and gone to school, where we were known by our parish and community, a place we thought of as home. So I started looking and looking. My eyes became well trained to see the For Rent signs. I called and visited many places, knowing what a hurdle lay ahead trying to rent a house for sixteen people with the worst possible credit rating. Where were we to go? What was to become of us? Was there no place open to us, no roof to cover our heads?

Just for a change of pace from being continuously discouraged at looking at small, old, and less than safe neighborhoods, I called a realtor who was showing a large new construction home for sale or rent in a perfect location in Frankfort with an exorbitant price. I arranged a house showing and together with my teenage daughter, Bridget, we took a look. As we were walking up the front sidewalk to the front door, a man and woman who were walking by the house called to the realtor to ask if they could see the house too. Well, that was awkward, but she said yes, and so they joined in on our house showing. We ignored each other as we went our separate ways looking around inside. The house was magnificent, and I knew the house would be perfect for us, but there was no way we could get it. As our showing ended, the man from the sidewalk looked me directly in the eye and eerily said to me as he walked out the front door, "This would make a wonderful home for you and your family." I never saw him before or since.

Well, I believed it would too! But again, I knew it was impossible. We certainly couldn't afford the rent, and even if we could, the owner certainly wouldn't rent to us! But, I told Jim about it, and we left it at that. Soon thereafter, we broke the news of our financial straits more explicitly to my father. He had been aware Jim's business wasn't doing so well, that our house was up for sale, but had no idea we were facing imminent foreclosure.

At this point, we were thinking we would need to move to our cottage in Michigan, a small vacation house we bought when the twins were one year olds after we had outgrown our pop-up camper. (Ten kids in a pop up and mom and dad was not going to work indefinitely.) I would need to homeschool the remaining nine school-aged children, and Jim would have to commute to and from his work in Chicago. My dad responded that we didn't really want to do that. He knew our life was here, our children were happy in the good private schools they were attending – also through God's providence – and being isolated and alone with the children most of the time with Jim away working out of state would be very hard. Yet, he did not offer any other suggestions but was clearly disappointed in us and for us. In any event, we weren't asking for help, just informing him of what was coming to pass.

Another sleepless night followed and then the next day, my dad called me. He offered to provide us with a "pre-inheritance" –

which was enough for us to rent the "perfect" house in Frankfort by providing six months rent in advance. It all looked like a go, and we continued to pack, and pray to God in thanksgiving. We arranged for the movers, and everything was set. Could this really be going forward? Was everything really going to work out? Then came the phone call from the realtor of our dream home. The owner had just received an offer of purchase, and needed time to see if it was a viable offer. Again, we waited in the cloud of unknowing, praying, hoping, trying to understand this turn of events, this time with all our possessions boxed up around us and no place to go.

The night before we were to move, another call came in from the realtor – the potential buyer was a fraud, her offer not financially sound, and we could get the house! And providentially, we've been here ever since – going on five years now – and it has indeed been a wonderful home for us.

A Tick for a Christmas Gift

The summer of 2007 before we moved to our dream house was a summer of highs and lows, and not just with the weather. As we were waiting for the death blow of foreclosure, we spent some time at our Michigan cottage as we usually do. Our first book had been published, and we were waiting for the delivery of the first copy. I'll never forget the beautiful summer morning when the UPS man stopped his truck at the end of our long driveway and walked through the two-hundred white pine trees to our front door, carrying a package from the publisher.

Our front lawn had originally been planted as a Christmas tree farm years before our cottage was built, then the trees had been left abandoned to grow as they would. Now they shoot up tall and skyward but because their roots are so shallow they need the sunlight and the rain from God and they need each other to survive. They grow closely intertwined with their branches interlaced for strength. If one white pine tree grew alone, it would surely tumble down at the first strong wind, but not so when they grow together and rely on each other to live. This is how God intends his beloved sons and daughters to live as well – relying on Him and each other for what is needed to live. The white pines always remind me that we can't do it alone either. It was a reminder I would need to remember.

As the UPS driver handed the package to me, I felt the way all first authors must feel – the thrill of seeing your very own book in print in your hands! We did our first book signing event at a faith and family conference, and all fourteen of our children were with us. We were so grateful that the story of God's intervention in our lives was being shared to console and encourage other families in their faith journey as well.

That summer, our little girl, Mairead, our twelfth child, was five years old. She was very active, and loved to play and be outdoors with the big kids, spending time in the forest of pines that surrounded our cottage. We called her the little monkey, and the beautiful one! At times during that summer, she would get uncharacteristically listless. All her energy went away and she would just want to lay on the couch. But then the next day she would seem to be better. Her lethargy would come and go. One day she complained her knee hurt. She was taking swimming lessons with the other children, and I thought perhaps she had injured it in the pool. It did look swollen, so I took her to the urgent care center in the larger town near our cottage. After doing some routine tests, they didn't see anything wrong with her, and didn't treat her.

A few weeks went by with the same pattern of lethargy, then energy, the other knee would swell, then the swelling would dissipate. I brought her back to the urgent care center again, still with no positive diagnosis. More time passed and the children went back to school. Some days Mairead was her old self, full of fun, and running and playing. There were days when Mairead wouldn't have the energy to go to school, and she would just want to sleep. The symptoms would come and go and most days she was fine. One morning however, she couldn't get out of bed but had to be carried to the couch. We called the school to see if she had injured her knees the day before in gym class. We called our primary pediatrician and brought her right to the doctor's office. This pediatrician had taken care of all of our children for the past eighteen years and we trusted him. After explaining all her symptoms and examining her, he told us he thought it might be childhood rheumatoid arthritis, a disease which would impair Mairead's mobility for life. He said he could be wrong and he would run some tests. We would know in a few days.

It was right before Christmas. Jim had just lost his second job due to lack of funding and his position was being phased out. We lost our health insurance. Our house was just foreclosed on and we had just moved to our rental home barely getting into it, and were unsure how long we were going to be able to stay. And now, our little girl was facing a life-long debilitating illness with no health care coverage once Cobra ran out. Again we turned to each other and to God for support. We knew we had to rely on our faith to keep us strong, and we just continued loving and hoping and praying for the best, knowing that whatever God's will would be, it would be best.

A few days later, the doctor called to say it was Lyme disease. Mairead did not have rheumatoid arthritis! She must have been bitten by a tick in the summer, six months ago, and the symptoms were so similar. But all it would take to cure Mairead was antibiotics! God is so good! What an incredible Christmas gift to us – to give us back the health of our child.

That Christmas was a memorable one as we began to witness the generosity of strangers, and of friends and family alike. Word had spread of our financial plight, and gifts began flooding in – gifts of food, gift cards, presents for the children, checks in the mail, cash in envelopes left in our mailbox, boxes of clothes and coats left by our doorstep – and it hasn't stopped. We are indeed living "a wonderful life".[3] God does provide, prayers are answered, people do care, and love does exist.

No Place Like Home

Being back in our hometown again, back at our home parish and the grade school that all the children had attended was like coming home after a long exile. Our exile had been a self-imposed one, where we thought the grass would be greener, but in all reality, there is indeed "no place like home."[4] Another lesson learned and God's providence again made manifest.

We settled into our new home and a new chapter of our lives. Our family began to thrive again. Fiona, Maura and Clare, in sixth and fifth grade, tried out for the school play, Annie Jr., and Maura at the age of ten landed the lead as Annie! This became the start of the children's enjoyment of participating in school and community musical theatre productions. We knew they could all sing because that is what they enjoyed doing to pass the time in the car, but who could tell which of the voices belonged to whom? We were tempted to tease them by naming our family the Littleton Family Singers after the family in the Sound of Music but knew they wouldn't go for it!

Jim and I became involved again in serving our parish, and the pastor who we'd known well since 1999 asked us to be part of the spiritual renewal committee for the 35th anniversary year of the parish. He asked me to serve again on the parish council, which I had done previously under the former pastor while expecting our eighth child, Fiona. Jim and I helped to make plans for a perpetual adoration chapel, I started a mothers group, *MomsMatter!*[5] offering spiritual formation, intellectual study of papal documents on marriage and the family and practical guidance and support to mothers. Both of us continued to serve the Church by giving talks on marriage and family life and the Catholic faith at retreats and parishes to adult women, men and married couples, and to offer spiritual guidance.[6] Our children continued to attend daily Mass together with us before school, we continued our daily prayer life as a family with nightly prayer and the family rosary, and we continued to focus on the formation of our children intellectually, spiritually, and practically.

Jim revised our Littleton Family Manual[7] incorporating daily chores suitable to the children's current ages and capabilities adapting to the changes each year made with older children leaving to go back to college and little ones becoming more able to help around the home. The children come and go, they go off to college, and come home again and we adjust. We miss them and we treasure even more the ones left still at home. Our children are such a gift to us and we treasure each one of them in their uniqueness.

Six months after our move, in May of 2008, Shannon, our oldest, graduated from college. We went down to Ave Maria University for the commencement and met the commencement speaker, Deacon Bill Steltemeyer, who helped found EWTN, Eternal Word Television Network, with Mother Angelica. At a reception afterward, we were introduced to him and he learned that Shannon is the oldest of our fourteen children. Jim casually mentioned that we wrote a book about our family, and he immediately told us he wanted us to appear on EWTN Live to tell our story. That would eventually take place a year and a half later in November of 2009, right after the biggest and most unexpected cross hit us, but more on that later.

One Day With Two Job Offers

With the publication of our first book and the promotion of it amongst Catholic groups, we were invited to do some speaking engagements both locally and at the diocesan level at marriage retreats, pro-life groups, and faith and family conferences. Catholic radio stations interviewed us, and international online news agencies like Zenit as well.[8] We began to see how our story impacted others by giving them hope and inspiration to be open to life, to raise their children with a stronger spiritual foundation, and to keep one's priorities - one's hierarchy of values[9] - in order by putting God first, spouse next, then children, then one's work or ministry. We were gratified even if one person grew closer to Christ, as that was the intent of the writing.

We continued to strive to keep our hierarchy of values in order as well. Balance was key. Jim's business started to do better, and we were able to make our monthly rent payments, having just enough to pay our bills but never any surplus. I continued to be a stay-at-home mother but started to think towards the future when it might be feasible to help bring in a little income to help when I could. In the fall of 2008, I spoke to the principal of our children's grade school and offered myself as a substitute teacher but was never called in until March of 2009. After my first day of subbing, the principal offered me a full time teaching job for the following year. I told him I would pray about it. That same day I received a phone call from the new pastor of our parish. He too offered me a job, one that I hadn't applied for and wasn't seeking which took me very much by surprise, as the Director of Religious Education. I told him as well that I needed to pray about it.

Two job offers in one day after being out of the full time work force for twenty-four years – was God telling me something? It turned out that yes, again, He was looking out for us, providing for us. Jim's health insurance coverage through Cobra was nearing the eighteen month expiration in June, just three months away. If one of us didn't secure full time employment with benefits by then, we would have no health insurance, as the cost of it through Jim's self-owned business was more than we could afford.

Jim and I decided I should take the job at the parish as it offered more of a fit for my talents and interests, and more importantly much more flexibility to be home with the children during the school day. Shealagh, aged three, would start preschool in the fall and I could work in the mornings and be home with both her and Brighde, now four, for lunch and the rest of the day. I would run the program once a week after school, some evenings and on Sunday mornings when Jim and the teenage girls were home to be with the family. I said yes, and took a leap of faith, trusting that this was God's will, and He would give me the grace to do it all.

He came through for us, as always. Our new health insurance policy kicked in on June 1st, 2009, the very next day after the old one through Cobra expired, providing a seamless transition. We had not coordinated this, but God did, and for a very good reason.

A Father's Love Like God the Father's Love

A few weeks later, on June 27, a week after my fiftieth birthday, my father died. It was a Saturday morning, and we were at our cottage. My Aunt Kay, my father's sister who I had been named after, drove down our driveway unexpectedly, and I thought she was there just for a nice surprise visit as she has a summer cottage nearby. Before she even reached me on the front porch, she told me that my dear father had passed away during the night. It was very hard news to take, and we both sat down on the front step, embraced each other and cried for our loss. My children and Jim stood around us and it was a moment I won't forget.

Although he had been very ill, this news was difficult to bear as my dad made it his business to keep very close to all of us, all of our lives. A wonderful, caring husband, father, educator, and friend, he is sorely missed by so many. I feel gravely sorry for those who have not been blessed with a good relationship with their earthly fathers as it may be hard to imagine God the Father in a good light based on the modeling of fatherhood one's own parent provides. My father gave me a very wholesome and healthy view of what God in heaven must be like. At times I do sense that my dad might still be taking care of us, interceding for us. And he would be doing just that if he is indeed in heaven along with my dear departed mother and all the saints in heaven, canonized or not, as part of the Church Triumphant. They would be interceding for everyone still here on earth.

At the small church in our cottage town, a banner hung behind the altar that summer. It depicted the face of the resurrected Christ and no matter where I would sit at the various times I would attend Mass there, it seemed to me the way the folds of the fabric fell, I could "see" my father's face in the folds, and it seemed that

Jesus was looking at him so tenderly and mercifully. Although no doubt my imagination, it did give me comfort and consolation as I grieved for him. Even now, as I write this, tears come to my eyes, and I miss him greatly still.

That was a hard blow. God had allowed us to be stripped of financial security, our home taken away from us, and now I lost my father, and both my parents were gone. My faith told me and I believe this to be true, that God doesn't cause suffering to happen here on earth, but He does allow it to exist and can indeed even bring good from it. God doesn't cause evil to happen, as He respects the gift of free will He has given to man, and that is what has brought suffering into the world – man's poor choices in using this gift from God – in choosing to turn away from God's love which always results in sorrow, disorder and emptiness.

This is not how God intends us to live. He loves us and wants us to be happy, united to Him. Our loving God continues to reach out to us in infinite mercy through the Holy Spirit who lives within us, calling us to conversion through the graces of the sacraments which are His invisible love made visible. He gently teaches us the right way to live through our experiences, through other people He sets in our path, and through the teachings of our Faith. He directs our path, and He directs mine, for which I am grateful.

The good that has come of these slow detachments from my securities has been that I rely more on God than ever. Instead of making me turn away from Him in anger or with blame, the purifications have only strengthened my reliance on Him who is always trustworthy. God wants us to put our security in Him alone, our Creator, and not to be inordinately attached to the things of this earth, His creations – the material things of this world and even our loved ones. The material created things of this earth God provides for us because He loves us, and they can bring us closer to Him. We can learn of God's goodness through His beautiful creation, we can see the face of God in loved ones and friends, and learn of God's charity through the charity shown us by our neighbor, and we are called to do the same.

The purification and detachment continued and still continues, as I pray it will all my life so I can be worthy of eternal union with Him. "Dream that the more you struggle, the more you prove the love that you bear your God, and the more you will rejoice one day with your Beloved, in a happiness and rapture that can never end." St. Teresa of Avila[10]

Four months after the death of my father, Jim went to see a doctor for a persistent cough that wouldn't go away. He was diagnosed with leukemia.

A Whole New World

Jim had a cough that wouldn't go away. It was flu season, mid-October, and our area had been hit with an epidemic of swine flu. Although he kept resisting, finally he agreed to go see a doctor after weeks of the cough, night sweats and times when he couldn't seem to catch his breath. A friend gave him a referral, and he went for a physical for the first time since he was eighteen. He didn't want to go to our local clinic, but wanted to see a doctor who was affiliated with a Catholic hospital in the event he needed to be hospitalized, a possible premonition.

The doctor was very thorough and ran many tests, including a CT scan and blood tests over a two-day period, Thursday and Friday. That Monday, she called Jim in to tell him that she was referring him to a specialist due to very high white blood cell counts. She indicated it might be mono, but she also mentioned and was the first to use the word leukemia as a possibility. The date was Monday, October 19, 2009.

That night, Jim and I researched leukemia on the internet. We knew then with certainty in our hearts that this was to be the diagnosis. Jim had all the symptoms and now we knew why. For years, even in his early forties, Jim would need to rest during the day, his energy levels spent. I couldn't understand it as I was the one who was up most nights with newborns and taking care of sick children over the years and I rarely took a nap. He seemed very healthy overall, had a black belt in karate, ran two marathons, exercised daily, managed his own business, served in ministry for the Catholic church, was constantly giving of himself for his family and others, so we just attributed his tiredness to stress, overwork and maybe staying too busy for his own good. But now we knew the real answer.

I went with Jim to the consult with the specialist the next day. As we parked in front of the address that the doctor gave us, we realized that the building was the cancer unit of the hospital. To see the words emblazoned above the door made what we were facing even more frightening as it started to all became very real. We were lead to a small examining room and were asked many questions by the cancer specialist. He had four or five doctors-in-training in the room with us so it was rather overwhelming. I began to realize that Jim's must be a very special case that these young future doctors had not yet been exposed to as they were all taking copious notes and trying not to look me in the eye. Eventually, the specialist revealed the official diagnosis, Chronic Lymphocytic Leukemia.

As we left his office, we were in a state of numb shock. It was too soon to even formulate any questions or come up with next steps. We needed a couple of days to just absorb this news – just the two of us. As we arrived home, we tried to pretend that everything was normal on the outside. I recall I went to coach Maura and Clare's speech club at their grade school, and even though I was bodily present, my mind was just not there. When alone together that night, we had time to start letting the reality hit us and we were afraid, but still trusting that somehow even this would turn out alright. We clung to our faith and each other, this time even more desperately.

The day after the official diagnosis, Jim went downtown to St. Peter's Church in Chicago and did a three hour general confession.[11] The next day he went in for more tests and an MRI. That weekend, we told the children from Shane on up, my siblings, and Jim's parents. It was very hard to make those calls, to hear our college-aged children's happy voices on the other line, then to break the news to them. We had to repeat the news fourteen times to our immediate family - Jim's parents, our siblings and our older children - over that weekend, and it didn't get any easier.

So began our entry into a whole new world - a new world of cancer.

Tying Her Dad's Shoes

Our daughter Colleen felt strongly the need to come home from college in Rhode Island to see her dad and be with him that week. It was fortunate that she did come home as we were to need her help and presence as events unfolded. That evening around midnight Jim began suffering sharp pains internally from his right kidney area on upward. He couldn't lay down, or even sit without intense pain. He was also convulsed with serious coughing spells and had been for the past couple of days. He had difficulty taking deep breaths due to the pain, and thought he might have pulled a muscle while helping our brother-in-law move my father's old upright organ into the foyer of our house earlier that day. He spent much of that night walking around the house to see if the pain would subside.

At six in the morning, which was Sunday, November 1, 2009, All Saint's Day, Jim told me we should call his doctor and I needed to take him to the emergency room. Jim was in such bad shape that he couldn't even bend to put his shoes on and tie them but Colleen had to do it for him. It was a scary moment for all of us as we had never seen Jim so helpless and so much in pain. It was the beginning of the time that was upon us for the children to help care for their father. The sight of our grown daughter on the floor tying her father's shoes was one that a mother doesn't easily forget. It was role-reversal time.

As we drove to the hospital, Jim could breathe only shallowly. Breathing deeply caused him intense pain. At the ER they did a CT scan and chest X-ray and we awaited the results, giving him pain medication while we waited. Three hours later we had the diagnosis – bacterial pneumonia in the lower lobes of both lungs. It was the first real crisis and hospitalization, and it came upon him less than two weeks after his diagnosis. Our pastor came and gave him anointing of the sick, prayed the apostolic pardon prayer, blessed him with a relic of Archbishop Fulton Sheen for healing and witnessed the signing of his impromptu last will and testament that he had me draft in the examining room of the ER.

He was admitted over night to the community hospital, but the doctors made it clear he was better off at home due to the rampant germs he was surrounded by in the hospital ward; he even had a sick roommate with multiple visitors. His release couldn't be done quickly enough for fear he would get worse being there. A deacon from our church visited and told him the same thing; he was better off out of there, and quickly. It was then that Jim and I realized he needed some very specialized care and the community hospital just was not the place for his long-term medical needs.

Jim was put on strong antibiotics, given a breathing machine to exercise his lungs with and sent home the next day. A few days later, we received an email from my cousin John, a doctor. He had heard through my sister about Jim's condition and advised we get in touch with the head of the blood oncology department at Northwestern Hospital in Chicago. His father, my uncle, had received excellent care there from this specialist for his leukemia a few years prior. John put in a call for Jim and less than half an hour later, Jim was on the phone with the specialist, and set an appointment for us to meet with him the very next day.

That morning, Friday, November 6, I woke up with a high fever. I was very sick, but also desperate to go with Jim to Northwestern to meet with the specialist. I had caught the same bacterial infection that Jim had due to being in such close contact with him. I was forced to realize I could not possibly go with Jim to the hospital so I reluctantly stayed home and tried to get better, and later that day received a prescription for antibiotics myself. Our oldest daughter, Shannon, accompanied him for the first consult. Jim came home with a greater hope. Jim's new doctor explained the three levels of gradual treatment for Jim's form of leukemia: first chemotherapy, then if that doesn't work he could try clinical tests, and as a last resort – a bone marrow transplant, perhaps ten to twenty years down the road. He made it sound easy and routine; that remained to be seen.

A Sidetrip to EWTN

It was very bad timing, but our appearance on EWTN was scheduled three days away. We had been invited to discuss our book *Better by the Dozen Plus Two*[12] on Fr. Mitch Pacwa's Wednesday night show, "EWTN Live" on November 11, and the next day to a taping with Doug Keck's "Bookmark" which would run during the month of May. We were both sicker than we've ever been in our lives with Jim recuperating from double pneumonia and I with the bacterial lung infection. We were too sick to even plan for what we would speak about, let alone even talk it over with each other. Even up to the night before we were to leave, we didn't really think we would even be able to get on a plane and do the interviews, but because we both really thought it was an opportunity to help others by sharing our story, we kept hoping and praying we would be well enough to go.

And so we did, and the Holy Spirit was with us. Although we didn't prepare, Fr. Mitch was such an excellent interviewer and made us feel so comfortable that the show went off quite well.[13] I held a cough drop clenched tightly in one hand and a Kleenex tucked in the other throughout the show. Jim only had to cough a couple times throughout the hour long show which was really quite miraculous in itself. Overall it was a delightful experience made so by the wonderful staff that made us feel so at ease.

No one but Fr. Mitch knew about Jim's diagnosis less than two weeks prior, and we all had agreed prior to going on the air not to mention it in the interview feeling that this new chapter of our story was just beginning to unfold. We did not want to overwhelm the audience with this news given our philosophy of life from a family of sixteen was already quite a bit to digest! The message we came to share was enough in itself, and by the incredible amount of feedback that started coming to us via email from around the world soon after the show ended, the message had been received just how and where God had wanted it by those who needed to hear it.[14] We were so very grateful that God had chosen to use us in this way, to make us both weak so He could fill us, making us practically incapable physically of the message coming from us alone so that it was from Him. He was filling us with what He wanted us to say since we were unable to do it on our own. It was His story to be told anyway, not ours.

Getting Our Ducks in a Row

A week after our return home, and one month to the day of Jim's diagnosis on October 19, Jim and I went to Northwestern to meet with Jim's doctor to hear the determination of the stage of his cancer and the treatment plan. It was not good news. The testing revealed that Jim had stage-four leukemia, the farthest advanced cancer, and a chromosome deletion which would make treatment especially challenging. The doctor did want Jim to start chemo nonetheless, and told us that a transplant was more surely imminent than twenty years out. He told us that a transplant could be swiftly started once all the ducks were in a row and it was time now to start doing just that – lining up those ducks. The chemotherapy would hopefully start reducing the disease in preparation for the transplant in the hopes of making the transplant successful.

We started learning and preparing fast. Jim's four siblings needed to be tested as possible donors as they were the best chance for a perfect match. We were told that there is a twenty percent risk of mortality with a matched sibling, meaning one out of five patients who receive stem cells from a sibling donor die in the process of the transplant procedure. We were then told that if the donor is not a matched sibling, the mortality risk is even higher. None of his siblings were found to be a perfect match. The search for an unrelated donor in the international bone marrow bank began, and it could take a while. It was a race against time.

In the meantime, we got our ducks in a row. We met with our accountant and our attorney. We had our wills drawn up. Jim and I discussed plans in the event he should die; how the business might be run without him, where I could live with the children, how our life insurance would help to provide for us once he was gone, where he was to be buried. He made me promise to keep raising the children the way we had been doing so together, close to God and counter-culturally. It was all seemed so unreal.

The chemo treatments and four-days-a-week visits to the hospital however were very real. His first cycle of chemotherapy started four days before Christmas, 2009 and continued through May of 2010. I rarely missed taking Jim to his treatments; perhaps twice a friend went with him when I couldn't miss a work commitment, as Jim would need and prefer my company and someone to drive him home the hour-long distance. I felt strongly that it was my place to be with Jim and I wanted to be there for him every step of the way. I did what I could to make that happen and I knew I had to rely on others to let me do just that. I accepted help. Friends would drive our children home from school, where Grace our daughter would be home to be with them, and mothers of our children's classmates soon started providing meals for us three times a week for which we were most grateful.

Despite all these rounds of chemotherapy over the course of six months, the disease was still rampant and the treatments were not successful. The aggressive cancer cells were winning out. Jim began to lose weight, his platelets dropped to way below normal, and he needed blood transfusions often. Many times during these months I had to bring him downtown to the emergency room where he ended up being hospitalized for various complications including severe skin rashes due to allergic drug reactions and for the return of pneumonia in his lungs. Often these crises would occur in the middle of the night, and we would end up sitting in the emergency room for hours before Jim was admitted. I was certainly gone more than I was home, rarely getting a full night's sleep, trying to juggle running my work life, taking care of my children, and caring for Jim. Fortunately our older daughters, Shannon, Tara and Grace lived at home with us, and one of them was always home for the children when they arrived back from school. They would prepare dinner, and be home with them at night while I stayed with Jim during his hospital stays.

Throughout all of this, Jim and I and all of our children continued to attend daily Mass, receiving our Lord in the Eucharist for strength and perseverance, relying on His grace and the prayers and help of so many - from our church, from our children's schools, from our family and friends, and from strangers - to keep us strong and hopeful. We knew that without Him and the help of others we wouldn't be able to get through this.

Our Last Remaining Hope

Ever since we knew the chemotherapy wasn't working very well, Jim had been researching clinical trials, spending considerable time on the internet over many months. Clinical trials are opportunities for qualifying cancer patients to try out potentially life-saving drugs as part of the process of getting them approved by the Federal Drug Administration. He recalled his cancer doctor's first conversation with him; one starts with chemo, then goes to clinical trials, then as a last resort, the stem cell transplant. We were already facing the transplant as soon as a donor could be found, and the chemo hadn't worked, so in the meantime, Jim went for a consult to St. Louis in June, he consulted long-distance with a hospital on the East Coast, and I went with him to San Diego for another consult. However, from the south and from coast to coast, he was rejected for a possible clinical trial. Our only last and remaining hope was the transplant.

In the early 1990s, twenty years prior, Jim had registered himself on the international bone marrow donor list, so when we finally received word that eight potentially viable donors had been found in the world, Jim himself was one of them, which reduced that number immediately to seven. Of those seven, considered by the medical experts to be a very small number, each had to be contacted to see if they were still willing and able. Of those seven, only two turned out to be viable prospects and thanks be to God, they both were perfect matches. We had a match and a spare. The doctors would determine the better of the two candidates, and we left it in their hands.

That summer of 2010, Jim had a reprieve from treatments as the medical team wanted him to try to regain some strength before the fall when they intended to try a more toxic treatment in the hopes of reducing the leukemia cells going into the transplant. The plan was to set the transplant for the first of the year. We treasured the time with the family that summer! We returned to our cottage in Michigan, spent the Fourth of July with friends, and the next day, I gave in to Jim's longtime wish to go on a driving pilgrimage to various shrines out east and in Canada.

I had been afraid of his weakness and poor health, and how we were to manage if he were to have a medical crisis so far from home with a van full of children and a trailer behind too! But I decided to have a little more faith, and do what would make Jim really happy. He wanted to visit the Shrine of the North American Martyrs near Albany, New York on whose feast day he was diagnosed, and he wanted to visit the Divine Mercy Shrine in Massachusetts, and the St. Joseph's Oratory in Montreal, that Blessed Andre Bessette (now Saint Andre) founded, both of whom Jim had always long been devoted to.

Putting his future, and ours, in our Lord's hands, entrusting the trip and Jim's health to Jesus, Mary, and St. Joseph, we set out on a spontaneous trip across country and into another that very afternoon! Jim and all of us thoroughly enjoyed the road trip and the visits to the shrines. It was a very blessed trip and we especially treasured a time of peace and relaxation together as a family, which was much needed and appreciated.

Day Zero

During the fall months and into December of 2010, Jim went through a series of toxic treatments to reduce the diseased cells so that the transplanted healthy cells from the donor could have a greater chance of fighting and taking hold. The treatments were especially hard, and Jim had to go to the emergency room and was hospitalized again twice for bad reactions and other complications. Bone marrow testing did show though that the diseased cells were decreasing, though not to a significant degree. There were patches of clean bone marrow, but still areas with fifty percent diseased cells. The doctors had hoped Jim could go into the transplant disease free, but that was not to be the case.

We enjoyed light in the darkness of that December when our daughter Tara became engaged to Ryan, a longtime friend from college. Tara is our second daughter and the first of our children to become engaged. The wedding was set for July 30, seven months away, and God-willing Jim would be six months post-transplant when he was to walk his daughter down the aisle! This hope gave Jim even more motivation to get healthy and to recover. We looked forward to the wedding day with great excitement and happiness as we recognize life does go on and each day is a gem to treasure. Here our daughter was finding her spouse and starting a new life with him, even while her dad underwent a life or death experience. We should expect that our interwoven lives will always be filled with times of peace, joy, pain and suffering which is the stuff of which life and love is made. It is in heaven that we will be truly happy.

Jim was admitted for the transplant on Tuesday, January 25, 2011, the Feast of the Conversion of St. Paul, to whom Jim had a very special devotion. The transplant took place three days later, during which time Jim received great doses of chemotherapy to completely eradicate his immune system so that his body would not fight off the new transplanted cells. Friday, January 28th, the Feast of St. Thomas Aquinas, was Day Zero, what is referred to by the transplant team as his birthday, the day he would receive new cells, and God-willing, a new life.

Day Zero dawned and Jim was in good spirits, ready to move forward and get on with it after the long wait for this day. The stem cells arrived fresh carried in a cooler, having been airlifted from a foreign country, from a still anonymous donor. The transplant itself consisted of an intravenous drip and involved no surgery. Jim was in no pain and had no complications. The process took less than two hours, and all went well. The medical team was incredibly kind and attentive as always, and Jim read Scripture when he wasn't joking with the staff. In Jim's words, the transplant itself was "a grace-filled time" and present in the room with him were myself, our daughters Shannon and Fiona, his leukemia doctor, the transplant team and a chaplain.

Over the next few days, things went along routinely. Nine of the children came to visit and we celebrated Brighde's fifth birthday in the hospital room with ice cream, then a little shopping trip to American Girl Place and the Disney store for gifts for her. We tried to make the experience of visiting Jim a happy, fun time for the children so as not to frighten them with the seriousness of what was really happening.

They were all mostly still so young, with our youngest Shealagh being only three years old, Brighde just five, Mairead seven, Patrick ten, the twins Maura and Clare twelve, and Fiona thirteen. Shane, age sixteen, was away at a high school minor seminary in Indiana but came home to visit that weekend at the hospital. Bridget, Deirdre and Colleen were out of state away at school, and Grace, Tara and Shannon, our college graduates, were home with us and helping so very much while I was with Jim.

During Jim's stay in the hospital, I spent my entire time with him, leaving only to go to Mass daily down the street to bring him Holy Communion, and for two brief visits home over the month of his hospitalization. The first few days I wondered if my help was really going to be needed as the staff was so efficient and the transplant seemed to be going along as expected, but I soon realized how very essential to his care that I be there for him, and that is where I wanted to be, nowhere else but constantly by his side.

Then the time of crisis was upon us. Jim was rushed in the night to the ICU with kidney failure.

On Our Way to Eternity

During the few days prior since the transplant a week before, Jim was steadily weakening. He was retaining fluids, and his appetite had decreased considerably. Due to the high doses of chemotherapy, he had severe mouth sores, and had tremendous difficulty sleeping. His voice when he spoke was very raspy and hoarse as he had dry mouth with no saliva since the chemo had killed off the production of saliva. They were pumping him with IV fluids to counteract the number of drugs in his system and to keep him hydrated; his blood pressure would alternate between being too high or too low.

When he would dose off, he would start speaking while in a dream state or semi-sleep state, and I would try to write down what he was saying. He seemed to be seeing people in his dreams that knew him, though he didn't know them. They would be calling him by his name, gratefully, families and other groups of people. There was a European man with his family who told Jim he was supposed to be dying but he was cured now. The man was jumping up and down with joy and Jim was telling the man to pray to Jesus Divine Mercy, He loves you very much. Jim himself was praying to have St. Faustina's spiritual life, as he had prayed in the past. He knows she suffered tremendously. Jim hoped he would get it cheap though. Jim said clearly "one way or another we are on our way to eternity."

In his dream state, Jim saw the book (I believe the book we wrote or perhaps the book he was to write)[15] and he had knowledge of how it was helping others. He seemed to be visualizing what would be done for others with the book. I wondered while I recorded his "ramblings" if he was "seeing" people that were being helped through his sufferings. I heard Jim "preaching and counseling" in his semi-sleep state and he was speaking normally and coherently which he couldn't do when he was really awake due to the dry mouth condition. Additionally he was so fatigued all the time that he would speak to me only very briefly and slowly when fully conscious. It was a remarkable thing to witness how clearly and normally he was able to speak in this dream-like state. He continued to say things like "it will all be ok in the long run. Jesus loves you now and always, Jesus Divine Mercy." He would pray through Divine Mercy and ask for tremendous graces for everyone.

From the very beginning of his visits to doctors and hospitals, Jim would ask everyone and anyone if they'd like a holy card. If they said yes, he would hand them a small Divine Mercy card, the size of a business card. These he would pass out to anyone willing to take one, and most people would. He was known throughout the cancer unit and in the blood bank as the distributor of the holy cards. He would always wear an Our Lady of Guadalupe pin on his lapel or shirt and a large St. Benedict crucifix around his neck.

Jim was often taken for the hospital chaplain and returning patients would ask for him to sit and talk with them as they received their chemo treatments. He had a calming, encouraging effect as one who had walked in their shoes and understood. Most times Jim would not let them know that he was just a cancer patient like them himself. He was passionate about helping others and giving them hope through their suffering. Jim would keep stacks of Divine Mercy cards on his bedside cart and when he became too weak to hand one out to the visiting cleanup person, nurse, doctor or anyone stepping inside his room, he would point to the cards to make sure that I asked them if they'd like one. Even to this day, if you went to this cancer unit, you can still see Divine Mercy cards on many people's desks. And so his ministry continues whenever a person might see the image of Jesus with his arms outstretched, and know God is with them, full of love and mercy.

Earlier that day, the kidney team had come in to do a CT scan and now came in to tell me that the amount of fluids and perhaps the combination of various drugs had lowered his sodium levels and his blood pressure as well causing possible kidney distress. His temperature was spiking, his breathing becoming more labored, and they were concerned that his kidneys were not working sufficiently to cope with the output needed to release the fluids and toxins accumulating in his system. His lungs were now affected and he had to be put on oxygen since they also found fluid in his lungs. They wanted to move him to ICU and put him on a kidney dialysis machine temporarily to release the fluid buildup until his kidneys could start working properly again. And so, they wheeled him away. It was 6pm on February 6th, 2011 – our daughter Mairead's eighth birthday and Superbowl Sunday.

Flowers in the Springtime

When I caught up to Jim in ICU with the rest of his belongings a short time later, I found him to be very unstable. The ICU team was unable to get any coherent answers from him so I was there to help give them the basics. The Superbowl had just started, I recall seeing it on the TV screens in other rooms, but it all seemed a world away from my reality for what seemed to be happening in this little room was scaring me to death. Suddenly a priest appeared and walked into Jim's little cubicle. Jim was able to ask him to hear his confession. It turns out the priest had arrived at the wrong room, which really was the right room for Jim. God provided Jim with the sacrament and a blessing. He was to need both before the night was out.

Besides Jim's unstable oxygen and blood pressure levels which currently were taking precedence in terms of crisis, the challenge to getting Jim hooked up to the dialysis machine was the fact that his platelets had dropped to only three thousand, with fifty thousand being minimally safe before spontaneous bleeding might ensue. Despite giving him several platelet transfusions, the levels did not increase. It was apparent that there was no safe way to make any kind of incision to insert a catheter line without taking on the life-threatening risk for Jim of uncontrollable bleeding.

That decision was put on the back burner, as another more immediate crisis was at hand. Jim's heart rate was skyrocketing, between 175 and over 200, and remained in that range for almost two and one half hours. The ICU team of doctors kept working on him, giving him heart medication to try to brake the surging heart rate. They had him hooked up to the defibulators, ready to go into resuscitation mode if necessary. I kept watching the numbers the entire time, praying for them to go down. At one point, Jim waved me over to his bedside and he said the words I hope never to have to hear again. He said his goodbyes to me, and gave me words of instruction to keep raising the children the way we had been. I could only shake my head in disbelief that this was happening. It was the worst moment.

Slowly over time, over a period of hours throughout the night, the heart medicine started working and his heart rate started to lower. By early morning, it had eventually come down to the 100 range. The medical team was still giving him platelets in preparation for the hopeful insertion of the catheter in order to start the kidney dialysis which had to be done. There was no choice. The risk had to be taken. They were going to move Jim to what they called a medical intervention floor to try inserting the catheter, and I was not allowed to go with him. This was another time of crisis. My sister Rosemarie came to be with me. I had sat up all night in ICU and now the day was dragging on with the time of the insertion continuously being postponed while we waited and prayed. I met a woman in the ladies room off the waiting room who had just lost her brother. I found myself holding her, crying along with her, consoling a complete stranger and it felt right.

Returning to my chair in the waiting room, I found my thoughts were racing. Was Jim going to make it? I could only keep imagining uncontrolled bleeding everywhere. What else was he going to be put through? For a year and a half he had endured the sufferings of powerful chemotherapies to no avail. Just days ago his entire immune system had been wiped out in preparation for the transplant, then he received donor cells and was in a precarious state as it was, his kidneys had just failed, he had almost died from heart failure, and now this. What was to happen next? I clung to hope and faith.

My sister distracted me and talked of flowers and springtime in her garden in Maryland, and I will always be grateful to her for that. It was the dead of winter in Chicago, we had just survived the worst blizzard in almost fifty years just a few days before, and she captured my thoughts with flowers in springtime.

I thought of all the other kindnesses that had come our way; my niece the medical intern who would come to visit often, the couple from church who came to visit Jim with she herself in failing health from cancer, my brother and sister-in-law who brought me lunch and cheered me up, those who kept in touch by calling me like my dear aunt who called regularly to give me encouragement, Jim's caring and wise mother full of good advice, my precious children who kept me grounded and strong for their sake, the many friends and family whose prayers and good deeds I could literally feel around me, the woman who later told me she would wake up unexpectedly at 3am during the nights of Jim's ICU stay and then would pray the Divine Mercy chaplet during that hour for Jim's recovery, the gifts and cards and blessed medals and relics that friends and people we didn't even know had sent us.

I felt surrounded by love and support even in this worst time of crisis, and that was what I thought of during that time and I was grateful to God. I was grateful to God for giving me Jim for the time I had him and for the children and the life we had shared together, a wonderful life, a blessed life. I realized that I could let him go if it had to be and I knew that God would give me the strength to go on.

Cutting Him Loose Of the Wires and Tubes

After some time had passed, and no one had come to tell me how the surgery went, I wandered back into Jim's ICU room and he still wasn't there. Soon however, a nurse came in to say it was successful! She had been with Jim the whole time, and had just left his side to hurry back to tell me the good news. I was so grateful for her kindness, and so very relieved! They had been able to insert the catheter with no bleeding. It seemed miraculous to me – how was that even possible?

And so Jim began to get better. The next day he left ICU, and was brought back to the transplant unit. Over the next twenty-one days, he continued to be sent over for periodic kidney dialysis. I would spoon feed him his meals, stay half-awake at night near his bed in case he needed anything, as he slowly gained back some weight and some strength to get back on his feet. His blood counts started to improve, and he began to get up out of bed and slowly learn how to walk again around the room and eventually around the halls with help. A physical therapist came to work with him, and Jim was very motivated to get better and to regain his strength. Even though the doctors thought he might need to keep going to outpatient kidney dialysis, he didn't need to do so after all. By the time he left the hospital, his kidneys had returned to full function – another miracle in my opinion!

The children were able to come to visit again, being sure to gown up and wear masks and gloves from head to toe, but to them it was a game and fun to do. Our three youngest daughters had birthdays during the twenty-eight days Jim was hospitalized, and we became adept at joining in on the partying at home via Skype from the hospital room. By the time Jim was permitted to be released, he was more than ready to go home. And home he went on Tuesday, February 22, 2011, the Feast of the Chair of St. Peter, and day 25 out from the transplant. He had been four weeks in the hospital, and had lost forty pounds, and with his six-foot-four frame, he looked like a skeleton. He had a long uncertain road ahead, but it was time to be reunited in person, in our home with our children. We were all ready, though we knew the recovery would continue with its challenges, we were now even stronger for the task ahead and so very grateful for the chance to start a new chapter together.

A Tall Walking and Dancing Skeleton

During the next few months, we lived very carefully. Jim needed constant care in a germ-free environment, and I learned to be a full-time nurse, even able to administer his IV medications over the first few days he was home. We had home nurses come in a few days a week to monitor and assess his progress. Jim was on a special diet, and was kept confined to his room. It was hard on the little ones who only wanted to be with him, but they had to gown and mask up and wear gloves again just like in the hospital if they wanted to enter our room. They wanted to sit on daddy's lap and just be with him, which they did!

Life slowly began to seem more normal. Jim was unable to drive, but was getting stronger and working hard to regain his strength by walking around the house with a walker. In the spring, he was strong enough to go outdoors and take walks alongside me down the trail in our town. He would always wear a hospital mask while out in public, we avoided crowds and when going to church, he would sit in the vestibule away from everyone. We had long ago cast aside any concern for human respect once we were on our fifth or so pregnancy. So we were not concerned about what people thought of us, therefore although the sight of Jim holding my arm looking like a tall walking skeleton, leaning on a cane and wearing a mask might look frightful to others, we were oblivious and just grateful for how far he had come. In fact, we didn't even notice the difference. He was just Jim, and dad, to us.

By the time of Tara's wedding, Jim was indeed able to walk her down the aisle, a bit frail still but without a cane! He did have his lovely daughter at his side to keep him steady! What a beautiful happy day! He had accomplished his goal and we all were so thrilled to see his progress. The day was just perfect. Jim moved all those in attendance at the reception by giving a most profound toast and prayer before dinner about what is truly important in life – true love which is total self-gift, of the bonds of marriage which continue to unite as time brings both sickness and health, his great gratitude for each precious moment of life, and the faces of his children which allow him to see God. Although still weak, he did dance with each and every one of his twelve daughters that night, and of course, with me! What a gift, to have all of us together, our two sons, all of our children, Jim's parents, our siblings and their spouses, and the many friends and family who helped us with their prayers and support to celebrate life and enduring love.

A Burning Candle Flame

Love is joy and pain. A sad lesson in this was brought home to the newlyweds just two weeks later, when Tara and Ryan were on their back deck enjoying a summer night having just returned from their honeymoon. I was awoken from a sound sleep by the telephone ringing and knew something was wrong. Ryan was on the line to tell me that Tara was involved in an accident and had burns to her hand and she was being taken via ambulance to the hospital. We found out the next morning that he had downplayed the seriousness of her injuries so as not to make us worry.

A tragic accident had happened when a liquid oil candle exploded creating a torch-like flame and Tara had literally caught on fire, resulting in third degree burns to her entire right arm, the side of her neck and upper thighs. Ryan saved her life by acting fast and putting her out, and Tara's natural instinct to cover her face protected her from burns there. She was rushed to Loyola's burn unit in Chicago and needed skin graft surgery and was hospitalized for two weeks. It was a very trying and frightening time but Tara and Ryan's love was so clearly evident as they too were there for each other through this trial and cross.

Tara's positive spirit that she was going to get through this and be just fine reminded me so much of the strength and courage that her father showed, but to see it in one so young, just twenty-four and just newly married with her whole life ahead of her was truly a witness. Never once did she complain, show pain or fear, but was strong and joyful through all she had to endure. My heart wrenched for her, as mother's hearts do feel the pain of their children. But she did not wince. Bravely she faced this cross with acceptance of God's will and I am so very proud of her. She still wears a pressure garment for the scarring, and will bear the scars all her life though they will fade, yet her heart is not scarred as she too has learned the mysterious lessons of what can be achieved through the cross if one bears it with Christ.

When We Give We Gather

One dark day that past winter while Jim was hospitalized for his transplant, my two sisters Maureen and Rosemarie insisted on taking me out to lunch nearby the hospital. At lunch they revealed to me their plan to host a fundraising benefit for our family to help with the financial difficulties they knew we were having. Jim had not been able to go to work for two years, from October of 2009 to October of 2011, although since he owned his own business he was able to hire a manager to run it while he did what he could to oversee it remotely. The burden of medical expenses, Jim's lessened income due to his illness and the costs of school and living expenses for our large family was an ongoing challenge.

My sisters asked me if I would let them do this for us. At first I really hesitated. It was hard for me to rely on others help as we had been brought up to be independent and self-sufficient by our parents who were educators. We had all earned advanced degrees and were prepared to be self-reliant. Though in reality, that was not truly God's plan for me or for anyone. God wants us to live in community with others (like the white pine trees), in charity and self-giving. We are called to be Christ-like to others, and to let others be Christ-like to us. God had taught me many lessons along the way teaching me to let go and to surrender to His will, not mine. He had taught me to rely on Him and those He sent to help me throughout my life. Hadn't I seen this over and over again? I certainly didn't want to forget the lessons and to suffer through relearning them! It was necessary in life to rely on others, to let others be generous, to humble myself so that others can show their love, for it is those who give who gather. We reap what we sow.

So I said yes. For the next eight months, February 2011 through October 2011, my sisters worked heroically to make the fundraising benefit a success, and it was! Over five hundred friends, relatives and strangers came together to volunteer or attend with nothing to gain themselves but everything to give. Old high school friends, old friends who had stood up in our wedding. people we had not seen in years but who all had somehow heard of this event for Jim came out in support and friendship. It was a tremendous celebration and it was really fun! We were overwhelmed by the generosity and outpouring of love. The donations were plentiful and helped carry us through a rough time financially, and took the strain of anxiety away. Our hearts were full of gratitude.

Healed Through Cancer

But they were to get even fuller! Two weeks after the benefit, and just over two years since Jim's diagnosis, on November 1st, 2011, All Saints Day, Jim was declared cancer free! The donor cells had completely taken over and had wiped out all trace of leukemia cells. If Jim stays cancer free for a three-year period, he can be declared cured.

Journeying through and surviving a life-threatening disease has made us realize most profoundly what a gift life is and each and every day of it should not be taken for granted. We knew with each child born to us that life is a profound gift, but we had more to learn. The life experiences over the past few years have taught us even more poignantly that every life is a gift, that every moment is a gem to be treasured. We have learned that God is faithful, that the love of family and friends endures, that love transcends pain and suffering and passing through it makes one stronger and more compassionate, more willing to forgive and show mercy and love. We take more pleasure in the little pleasures of life like time just being with each other, like serving and sharing our faith with others, and the lessons God has taught us along the way for His glory. We have truly been healed through cancer, healed in body and spirit in so many ways.[16]

We have all of us – all sixteen of us – been through this journey, not just Jim, as have all those friends and family and strangers who accompanied us along the way with their thoughts, prayers and support. All of you each in your own way have saved Jim's life, and given my life, my spouse, back to me. You have given our fourteen children their father back to them. You are the Mystical Body of Christ. We give our utmost thanks to all of you and to the incredible medical team, and the donor we don't even know – the man who gave of his own life blood to give life to a stranger, a truly Christ-like act.

We pray we can live the rest of our lives doing the same for others.

Epilogue

Jim: As of this writing in the summer of 2012, Jim has continued to get stronger and healthier. His skin has continued to recover from the ravages of the graft-versus-host disease that caused rashes and mouth sores. His blood counts continue to improve, the doctors are slowly weaning him off many of the maintenance medications, and he visits the hospital only once a month now for regular appointments and blood draws. His weight has returned, and he walks over two miles daily, while recently even participating in a 5K run with the children – coming in last, but as he says, the last shall be first! He has returned to his work pursuits, completed his book, *Healed Through Cancer,* and has revitalized his sense of humor and zest for life. He is happiest while spending time enjoying his family, watching them enjoy life as well, living each moment and treasuring it to the fullest.

Kathleen: I continue to work as the Director of Religious Education at St. Anthony's parish in Frankfort, IL and do part-time case work for the marriage tribunal of the Diocese of Joliet. I look forward to starting my second year pursuing a Masters in Theological Studies from the Institute of Pastoral Theology of Ave Maria University which I attend through an intensive weekend once a month from August through May. With Jim, I continue to speak on marriage and family life at parishes and at retreats, and we both continue to give spiritual guidance to those who seek it. My most enjoyable time is spent with my husband and children every moment of which I treasure as a gift from God. I also enjoy designing original antique reproduction samplers (www.crosssstitchantiques.com), and reading - my favorite fiction authors are J.R.R. Tolkien, L.M. Montgomery, and Sarah Orne Jewett.

Shannon: For four years now, Shannon has worked as a personal secretary to Cardinal George of the Archdiocese of Chicago. She will complete her Masters in Biblical Theology Summa Cum Laude from John Paul the Great University this fall, having obtained her Bachelor's Degree in Literature from Ave Maria University near Naples, Florida. She enjoys singing in the church choir, reading, and is an expert knitter.

Tara: With her husband Ryan, Tara has just celebrated her one year wedding anniversary. She continues to heal in both body and spirit from her burn. She has worked for the past two years as a preschool teacher at Noonan Academy, the excellent private independent Catholic school that her younger siblings attend in Mokena, Illinois. Tara also graduated from Ave Maria University with a Bachelor's degree in Literature. Ryan works as the manager of Jim's insurance adjusting firm, Littleton Claims Service, Inc. and they both look forward to starting a family of their own in God's time.

Grace: Having lived in Florida for the past year working at a Montessori preschool and obtaining certification in Montessori education, she will be returning home to the Chicagoland area this fall to work as a Montessori teacher at an Academy in downtown Chicago. She looks forward to living downtown with her sisters, Shannon, Colleen and Deirdre in a beautiful apartment with views of Lake Michigan.

Colleen: After discerning a religious vocation for the past five years in Rhode Island while obtaining her Bachelor's degree in Pastoral Studies with Honors, she has returned home and will be starting a new phase of her life by pursuing graduate studies in English Language and Literature at Loyola University of Chicago. She hopes to continue towards a doctorate degree to become a professor and bring her love for the art and beauty of literature to others.

Deirdre: This fall Deirdre will also start graduate studies in English at Loyola in Chicago and will continue to write for literary journals, with the goal to become a published writer and teacher at the high school level or higher. She obtained her Bachelor's in Literature from Ave Maria University Cum Laude, while being very involved in student government. She enjoys reading, cross-stitch, traveling and time with friends and family.

Bridget: This summer between her junior and senior years of college, Bridget has worked as an intern in Washington, DC for the Heritage Foundation, a conservative think tank. She is a Politics major and is considering law school or graduate studies in international relations. Bridget enjoys ballet, tennis and traveling and spending time with her friends and family as well.

Shane: After attending a high school minor seminary while discerning the priesthood, Shane will be starting at the college seminary for the Archdiocese of Chicago this fall. He is an active young man who enjoys all kinds of sports and values the spiritual life. He has survived his childhood growing up with twelve sisters and is charitable, polite, and intelligent with a great sense of humor.

Fiona: This fall, Fiona will be continuing her high school years as a Junior at St. Ignatius College Prep in Chicago. She as well as her younger twin sisters obtained an academic and financial scholarship making it possible for them to attend this fine institution, another gift from God through the generosity of others. She especially enjoys Advanced Placement History and Classical studies, competing in Latin and Greek competitions for fun. Fiona is very motherly and kind to her younger sisters, creative, organized and an avid reader.

Maura: Along with her twin sister, Clare, Maura will be continuing her high school years as a Sophomore at St. Ignatius. She is outgoing, warm and full of life, and especially enjoys singing and participating in musical theatre, improv and drama in school and in community productions. Maura as well as all the children, takes wonderful care of her dad, seeing to his needs, and spending time in his company.

Clare: With her twin sister, Maura, Clare will continue at St. Ignatius as a Sophomore this fall. The most athletic of all the Littleton girls, Clare enjoys running and outdoor activities. She is especially devoted to the family dog, Collette, a Shetland sheepdog. Clare too enjoys acting and has landed roles of a comedic nature in school and through community theatre.

Patrick: Along with his only brother, Shane, Patrick continues to cope well with living with twelve sisters, holding his own and staying tough while often instigating tears from his very feminine little sisters who don't appreciate his rough-housing nature. He will be entering seventh grade at Noonan Academy this fall where he is an excellent student, enjoying drama club, community theatre, and school athletics. He has probably grown a foot this past year, and joins the club of being taller than his mother now along with all his older siblings.

Mairead: Still retaining the nick-name of the Beautiful One, Mairead at age ten is a slender, active, gentle girl. She loves ballet, reading and playing with her little sisters. She too enjoys singing and performing in plays and community theatre, recently landing the role of Marta in the Sound of Music, who wants a pink parasol for her birthday.

Brighde: At age seven, and starting second grade this fall, she along with her little sister will forever be called one of the babies of the family. A sweet little girl, affectionate and loving, she is a joy to be with, full of conversation and engaged in all the going-ons of her large family. She enjoys her friends, her dog, and anything to do with princesses.

Shealagh: Although the baby of the family, she is probably smarter than all of us put together and is very precocious for a six-year old. She has been able to outwit all of us with her mental capabilities leaving us in the dust wondering where on earth she learned all she knows! She is active, endearing and along with Mairead and Brighde, is daddy's special little girl.

We truly are blessed and rich in children of all shapes, sizes, ages and varieties! Each one of them is a treasure to behold.

They are indeed our life and our legacy.

Always the proud papa with baby #14 February 2006

Our fourteen children February 2006

Brighde and Mairead September 2006

Our 25th Wedding Anniversary August 2008

Our 14 children in the summer before diagnosis August 2009

Jim with the children in the summer before diagnosis August 2009

Our fourteen children just before Jim's transplant Thanksgiving 2010

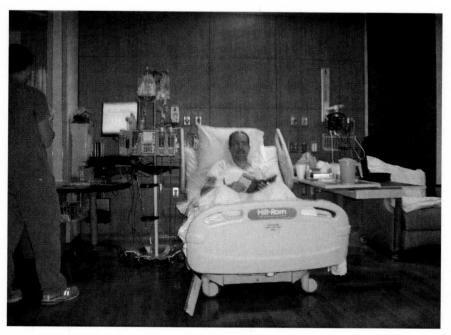

Jim during stem cell transplant January 28, 2011

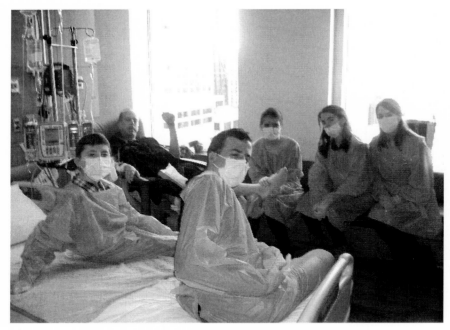

Our children visiting their dad in hospital February 2011

Our two boys July 2011

Our twelve girls December 2011

Entire family at Tara and Ryan's Wedding July 30, 2011

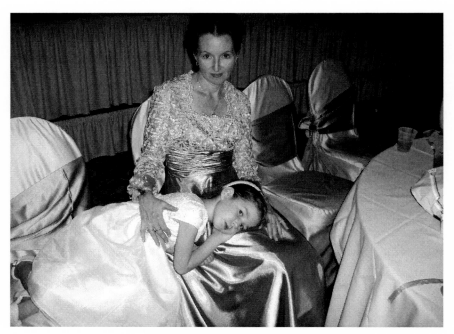

Our youngest and me at end of reception July 30, 2011

A toast to health, happiness and holiness Christmas 2011

The back of our full size van gets lots of attention Summer 2012

Appendix

Appendix Contents:
MomsMatter! Materials
Selected Talks Published and Delivered by Author 2000-2011
Littleton Family Manual Contents
Emails Received After EWTN Appearance

Promotional Flyer for MomsMatter!

Here's a new opportunity to grow in your faith and
form friendships with other Catholic moms of all ages.

M.O.M.S. Matter!
Mothers Offering Mentoring and Spirituality
~ by mothers and for mothers of all stages & ages ~

M.O.M.S. Matter! offers support, fellowship,
intellectual stimulation,
and faith formation for women in their roles as mothers
at all ages and stages of motherhood.
The twice-monthly sessions will include social time
and refreshments,
speakers on topics of interest to Catholic mothers,
sharing and networking of ideas and best practices,
gospel reflections,
and study of the Church's teachings on the Dignity of Women*.

Testimonials from Members!
"The MOMS group provides an opportunity for me to learn more about
and reflect on my faith, find support in my daily faith journey, and offers
easy, practical, ready-to-implement suggestions that bring peace into my
soul and my home, and deepens my personal faith." DJ

M.O.M.S. Matter! meets each second and fourth Tuesday
9am-11am in the Padua Center
Babysitting provided at $5 per child.

Join us and realize the fullness and beauty
of our vocation to motherhood!

Please contact Kathleen Littleton at __ - ___ - ___ or at
klittleped@aol.com
for more information and to register.

Program sponsored by St. Anthony's Parish Spiritual
Renewal Committee

*Study materials published by FamiliaUSA, an affiliate of Mission
Network, a Service of Regnum Christi

Overview of MomsMatter! Meetings

M.O.M.S. Matter!
Mothers Offering Mentoring and Spirituality
~ by mothers and for mothers of all stages & ages ~

Why:
• to offer support, intellectual stimulation, fellowship, and faith
formation to mothers of all ages as we live out our
vocations as Catholic mothers
• to build relationships, to grow in our faith, be a witness to other
moms, share and network … to be hearers, bearers and
sharers of the faith!
• to help moms appreciate their role as mothers as more rewarding
and challenging as any career, and much more pivotal in terms of
getting to heaven! It's our God given responsibility and privilege;
our unique, nontransferable mission.

Who:
• For all women - mothers or not - and of all ages and stages, new
moms, grandmothers, godmothers, spiritual mothers,
mothers-to-be someday!
• Open enrollment! Keep inviting friends!
Come and join in anytime!

What:
• Bible
• Catechism of the Catholic Church
• Dignity of Women Book

When:
• To meet twice a month at Padua Center
• second and fourth Tuesday mornings 9-11am with
babysitting @ $5 child

How:
Second Week of the Month:
• Speakers and Sharing – moms to moms – fellowship
and formation

Dates:
10/14, 11/11, 12/9, 1/13, 2/10, 3/10, 4/14, 5/12

Fourth Week of the Month:
• Discuss Authentic Feminism – John Paul II's Dignity of
Women document
• Dates: 10/28, 11/25, 12/23 no meeting,
1/27, 2/24, 3/24, 4/28, 5/26

Moms Matter! **Agenda For Each Session:**
9:00-9:15 Social Time and Refreshments
9:15-9:45 Opening Prayer, Gospel Reflection and Faith Formation
9:45-10:45 Week Two Speaker and Topic Discussion
9:45-10:45 Week Four Document Discussion Dignity of Women
10:45-11:00 Resolution and Closing Prayer

Opening Prayer
Leader: Come Holy Spirit,

All: Fill the hearts of your faithful and enkindle in them the fire of your love.

Leader: You send forth your spirit and things are created;

All: And you renew the face of the earth;

Leader: Let us pray: Oh God, you taught the hearts of your faithful people by sending them the light of your Holy Spirit. In that same Spirit give us right judgment and the joy of your consolation. We ask you this through Christ our Lord. Amen

All: Amen. Hail Mary, full of grace ...

Closing Prayer
Leader: We give you thanks, Almighty God, for all your gifts, you who live and reign forever and ever.

All: Amen. Hail Mary, full of grace ...

Questions? Contact Kathleen Littleton (__-___-____) klittleped@aol.com

Schedule for MomsMatter!

M.O.M.S. Matter!
Mothers Offering Mentoring and Spirituality
~ by mothers and for mothers of all stages & ages ~

October 14, 2008: Balancing Our Roles as Wives, Mothers and Baptized Catholics
• Being a Woman of the Eucharist – Prayer Must Come First
• Organization and Home Management
• Time Management for Catholic Moms – juggling Many Schedules and Hats
• Delegation of Responsibilities
• Computer Skills for Busy Moms
• Tackling Paperwork

October 28: Dignity of Women Study Lesson 1

November 11, 2008: Relating to Our Closest Relations - Our Husbands and Our Children
• Strengthening Marriage – spousal communication
• The Five Love Languages
• Understanding Temperaments

November 25: Dignity of Women Study Lesson 2

December 9, 2008: Extended Family Challenges
• How to balance different faiths within the family
• How to evangelize your own siblings and extended family
• What to do when kids (younger and older) reject the faith

Dec 23, 2008: No Meeting

January 13, 2009: Health and Fitness – True Beauty Inside and Out
• Fitness and Nutrition for Busy Moms and Families
• Skin Care
• Exercise for Beginners with Passion and Prudence
• Breastfeeding and Catholic Motherhood
• Modesty – Pure Fashion for Girls and Women

Jan 27, 2009: Dignity of Women Study Lesson 3

February 10, 2009: Raising Christian Children in an Unchristian World
• Motivating kids to give God their best in School
• Positive motivators to get kids to cooperate
• Teaching self-confidence/helping others less confident
• Homework Helpers
• Teenagerism
• Finding support amongst like-minded families

Feb 24, 2009: Dignity of Women Study Lesson 4

March 10, 2009: Understanding the Meaning of Suffering
• Handling personal health issues and keeping going as a mom
• Relying on our Lady, the Blessed Mother, the Ideal Role Model
• Miscarriage and Infertility
• Staying rooted in the faith despite turmoil in the family

March 24, 2009: Dignity of Women Study Lesson 5

April 14, 2009: Parenting Challenges
• Getting your preschooler child ready to attend school
• Decreasing your child's negative behavior
• Raising Special Needs Children – ADD/Hyperactivity
• Adoption
• Coping as a member of sandwich generation
• Relating to Adult Children
• Choosing schools/colleges

April 28, 2009: Dignity of Women Study Lesson 6

May 12, 2009: TBD

May 26 – Dignity of Women Study Lessons 7 and 8 and Last Meeting of the Year

Talks and Writings Published Or Delivered by Author, Years 2000-2011

No Regrets For Being Open To Life
Like Mary, Be a Woman of the Eucharist
Raising Christian Children in an Unchristian World
First the Woman, Then the Saint: Living a Life of Balance
Prayer: How and Why to Do It
Becoming One With the Creator (Not the Created): How to Practice Catholic Meditation
Spiritual Direction: The Why's and How's
What Is Love? Total Self-Giving
Zeal for Souls: Living Our Baptismal Call

No Regrets For Being Open to Life
Published on Catholic.net, 2008

By Kathleen Littleton

Have you ever thought how attractive the example of Our Lady must have been when she was caring for the Christ Child? Although scripture has left us little if any of the words of Mary, artists have rendered Mary caring for Jesus. In those famous portraits, we see her peacefully and lovingly holding or teaching her son. How many women of her day, watching her with Him, would want to imitate her gentle and loving ways? They didn't know her secret, that she was caring for the Savior Himself. But she did.

As mothers today, we need to remind ourselves that we too are caring for Christ in each of our children. The gospel tells us that whatever we do for the least of His little ones that we do unto Him (see Matthew 25:40). We too, like Mary, are called to be as gentle, loving and patient as she was with Him. As we try to imitate the virtues of Mary, keep in mind that we too need to be a witness to others of these virtues. Our example as we care for our children will either repel or attract.

Perhaps you've been in a store or restaurant when a child is not having a good moment. Naturally everyone's eyes dart that way to see how the situation will be handled. Perhaps you, like me, have been the mom of that child! You are aware others are watching. Now is the moment to be the witness God is asking you to be, the witness like Mary of patience and gentleness. In today's anti-life culture, children are often seen as a burden and not a gift. Often times, the reaction parents get from others is a judgment, and not a good one. People will watch us and judge us, even when our children are being good! Often they will judge us for the simple fact that we have children. We need to ask ourselves why the world can be so critical of one of the most natural aspects of life, to have a child. I contend that the reactions one gets aren't so much a reflection on you, but reveal a hurt within the one doing the judging.

Recently I heard a story of three moms who were enjoying lunch at McDonalds with their toddlers, about six of them, who were happily playing and being very good. The moms were engaged in light conversation. They couldn't help but notice that at the next table, one woman kept looking over at them with a frown on her face. One of the little boys kept turning around to look back at her and smile at her. The mom of this little boy finally asked him what he was doing. He said, "I'm just trying to make her smile."

Eventually this woman asked the group of moms if all the children were theirs, in a somewhat critical sort of way. The mom of the little boy said yes, but we actually have more children. She went on to explain that her little son was the youngest of seven, that this mom next to her had ten, and the other mom present was expecting her ninth. At that, the woman exclaimed, "What! Are you crazy!" Then, she stopped herself, and paused. Suddenly, tears came to her eyes and she said, "And God is taking care of you, isn't He?"

Having opened up, she then told the group that years ago, she had decided after two children that she had had enough. She closed herself off to life, even though her husband wanted more. She wanted to be in control, to pursue her career, to have the security of being in charge of her life and her future. A few years later, her husband died suddenly at the young age of 29. She had regretted her decision ever since, but it was too late.

As for the young moms, they are practicing Catholics who know the Church's teachings. They know that God is in control of every aspect of our lives. They know by following the Church's teachings on openness to life, that God will give them a child if it is in His plan, and if He does, He who created that child will sustain that child! There is nothing to fear.

Our only fear as Catholics is that out of selfishness we will not have the children God intended to give us from before time existed, the children that God had thought of from before they were even created. "Before I formed you in the womb, I knew you…" (Jeremiah 1:5). These children each have their own unique mission in life to make our world a better place. They are not a burden, but a gift.

Let us not let the lies of our culture make us deny God anything. Be not afraid. With Him, we will have no regrets!

Copyright 2008

Like Mary, Be a Woman of the Eucharist
Published on Catholic.net, 2008

By Kathleen Littleton

We all know our mission as baptized Catholics is to know, love and serve God in order to be with Him in heaven. But HOW do we come to know Him? Like the disciples on the road to Emmaus, it is in the breaking of the bread, the Eucharist (see Luke 24:13-35). It is by receiving Him and spending time with Him eternally present for us in the Blessed Sacrament that we come to know and love Him. It happens supernaturally. It happens through graces we cannot see, touch or feel, but it happens nonetheless if we believe and open our hearts to receive what He longs to give us.

But again, the question arises how do we as busy women - single women, married women, college age women, working women, stay at home moms, all of us women - find the time amongst our myriad daily duties to be like Mary, a woman of the Eucharist?

Put Him first. Everything else will fall into place according to His will. Don't try to fit Him in later, in your leftover time. It won't work. You won't do it.

Live your life by a hierarchy of values: God first, then spouse, then family, then work/ministry.

Through the Eucharist, God will infuse His graces into us so that we come to know and love Him more. But knowing and loving aren't enough. We also are called to serve Him by sharing our love for Christ with others.

The Catholic Church provides us with four beautiful ways to live a Eucharistic life. Let's look at one of them now, then in a future column we will look at the other three and how we can serve Christ by sharing Him with our neighbor.

☐ Eucharistic Celebration

Frequent attendance and participation at the Eucharistic celebration and reception of the Holy Eucharist, more often than once on Sunday, even daily if possible, will transform you supernaturally. Make the commitment and God will do the rest. He will give you the graces to want to persevere. Just start.

And do "let the children come to me, and do not prevent them..." (Matthew 19:14). Our children receive graces even though they don't understand what is happening. Do we truly understand this sublime mystery? Liken it to being out in the sun, feeling the rays and the warmth. Is it conditional on understanding the science behind how it works? Do bring your children to Mass with you, and don't let the human respect factor hinder you. Don't fear that your children will disturb others. God understands. He is the one that has given the children to you in the first place, and He wants them there, that is all that matters. Over time, our children adjust to coming as a natural and expected part of their day.

☐ Eucharistic Hours

Time spent before the Blessed Sacrament exposed in an adoration chapel for a "holy hour" for any period of time will also give you graces to know, love and serve God more fully. You will be given peace and encouragement to continue your walk with Him. You will feel an overwhelming sensation of God's mercy and personal love.

Before the tabernacle is where a woman of the Eucharist brings her troubles, concerns, joys, blessings and sorrows to share with Christ. It is a place where she will find perfect rest and comfort, like the fullness of an infant after a feeding.

What should one do there? You can do some spiritual reading, pray the rosary, pray for your needs and those of family and friends, pray for the Church, pray for vocations. Or you can just adore Him; be with Him. As an old man who would sit for hours in church reportedly told St. John Vianney, the Cure of Ars, in response to his query as to what he was doing every day just staring at the tabernacle, "I look at Him and He looks at me."

How to fit it in? Some women sign up for a set hour each week, some even in the middle of the night. Others routinely go at the same time each week. Start slow, go for a few minutes if that's all you can do. God will lead you to more over time. He will help free you up to spend more time with Him. Be generous with Him. He will pay you back abundantly as he cannot be outdone in generosity.

☐ Eucharistic Visits

Stop into a Catholic church briefly on the way home from work, between classes, on your lunch hour, before picking kids up from school. Give Him your day, your activity, your concerns, your hopes, your projects. Put it all in His hands. Make it His work.

When you drive by a Catholic church be aware that you are passing the Blessed Sacrament. Make the sign of the cross. Unite your will to His. Make a spiritual communion.

☐ Spiritual Communion

By offering up a spontaneous prayer in your heart, you can unite yourself to Christ throughout the day, to do His will, for His glory. Tell God how much you wish you could receive Him in the Eucharist, but cannot at this time, but you desire nonetheless to be spiritually united to Him. It can go like this:

"My Lord, Jesus Christ, I love you with all my heart and I ardently desire to receive you in Holy Communion. Since I can't receive you sacramentally at present, so come at least spiritually into my heart as if I were receiving you. (Pause) I love you and unite myself to you. May I never be departed from you. Amen."

As baptized Catholics, we are the instruments God has chosen to awaken in many people their hope, enthusiasm for the faith, and love. We are the tools Jesus needs to reach many men and women who seek and await him, sometimes unknowingly. He also has wished to need us to slake the immense thirst for God that people today suffer from.

Our degree of faith and love conditions the generosity of our response, our ability to say with Mary that He can count on each one of us. "Behold, I am the handmaid of the Lord. May it be done to me according to your word" (Luke 1:38). "Here I am, Lord, send me" (Isaiah 6:8). Let us ask ourselves: am I aware of this reality, and am I embracing and living out this responsibility?

Let us ask Christ to make us women of the Eucharist, to inspire us with the grace of knowing how He wants us to serve Him, and to give us the grace, strength and perseverance to carry out the unique and personal mission He chose for us before we were born. What we give to God with a loving and humble heart can never be considered a waste. Anyone who has tried it knows how very soon, perhaps without being aware of it at first, surprising changes happen in one's life. Take time to reflect on the changes that may have occurred in your life as a result of being a woman of the Eucharist. Think about the changes you desire will still occur by uniting yourself more closely to Christ in this way. Ask Him to make this happen. Ask Him to make you love Him more. He will!

Personal Questionnaire
A Woman of the Eucharist

1. Do I really feel that God loves me? Can I reflect on an experience of God's personal love and mercy towards me?

2. When I think about the incarnation, passion and death of Christ, am I moved to respond in love and gratitude?

3. How have I responded to God's love for me in my life? Have I been generous in my response, in my self-giving love to God and to others in my life? What concrete acts of love have I performed out of love for God toward my neighbor?

4. Do I try to receive Jesus Christ in the Eucharist as often as I can? Do I have faith in the real presence of Christ in the Eucharist? Do I believe as the Catholic Church teaches, that this is truly the Body, Blood, Soul and Divinity of Jesus Christ and not just a symbol? Do I realize the graces that await me by increasing my Eucharistic devotion?

5. Is the giving of thanks after communion routine and boring, or is it a loving dialogue with Christ? Do I reduce it to a series of self-centered petitions? Do I listen to Christ in these moments?

6. Do I genuflect to Christ with a spirit of love and adoration or has it become a reflex?

7. During times of prayer, do I try my best not to be distracted even when faced with adverse circumstances?

8. Do I seek to know and love God more by spending time with Him in prayer and the reading of scripture? Do I try to make a visit to Christ in the Eucharist by

stopping in at a church even for a few moments during the week?

9. Am I willing to make more time for God by committing to a holy hour of adoration? Might God be asking me to make time in my life to continue to form myself as an authentic Catholic by joining a parish faith formation program?

10. We are challenged to hand over to God the reins of our lives, our families, our efforts for holiness and our good works, and we too will see the marvels He will work through us. Reflect whether or not I have yet done so. What might be holding me back? Form a resolution to become a woman of the Eucharist and take steps to make it happen this year.

Raising Christian Children in an Unchristian World – Outline Of a Talk

☐ 'Train a boy in the way he should go; even when he is old, he will not swerve from it." (Proverbs 22:6).

☐ To raise is to form.

☐ As parents, God has given each of us the responsibility, but also the graces, to be the primary formators of our children.

☐ We can't delegate this to anyone, not a caregiver, a grandparent, a babysitter or a teacher.

☐ As Catholic parents trying to raise our children to be leaders for the Church in today's society, our families need to live in the world, but not be of the world.

☐ We need to take the narrow path that leads to life, eternal life, even when, and especially when it means not doing what everyone else is doing.

☐ **Integral Formation: Spiritual, Human, Intellectual, and Apostolic (Service/Ministry)**

☐ **Spiritual Formation: A Eucharistic Life** – this is where it all starts for our family
- o Daily mass as a family for years
- o With all the little ones too
- o Weekly confession
- o Evening family rosary with children taking turns leading
- o Older ones read gospel passage and lead reflection
- o Program of life for each child geared to his/her age
- o Based on a virtue
- o Example: of our three-year-olds' program of life:
  - Was I nice to my baby sister today?

- Was I good in church?
- Did I suck my thumb too much today?

o Spiritual guidance appointments with Dad for older ones regularly

o Visits to Christ in the Eucharist on way home from work and school

o Weekly holy hours for mom and dad, taking a child or two with us once in a while

o Sundays are a day of rest - no homework either:

o And our children attend demanding schools that give a lot of homework

o They find a way to get it done on the other six days God gave them to do it in

☐ Human Formation: Form Virtuous Children

o Modest clothing is a must: our bodies are temples of the Holy Spirit

o Good manners: on the phone, to adults, look them in the eye, speak up, be direct and polite

o Use extreme caution with TV, movies, and music

o About six years ago we got rid of cable connection and antennas and have never missed it

- It's totally freeing
- We still watch a movie with our VCR and DVD as a family integration activity on weekends
- Our children are experts and connoisseurs of the classic family movies from the 1930s to the present day

o Apply critical thinking to the media in family discussions

o Encourage obedience that is immediate, joyful and done well.

- Complaints mean the work is doubled.

- Will my kids still love me? Yes!
- Use positive motivation and swift forgiveness

o Charity and unity key virtues
- No raised voices; speak softly, think kind thoughts
- All for one and one for all: learn to share fast in a large family
- Our children always ask for "one more for my younger sister"

o They learn to think less of self – more of others
- Example: one of our five-year-old twins won an award the last day of school.
- When the other twin was asked how she felt about her twin sister winning the award,
- With absolutely no jealously, she responded with a big smile, "I was just so happy for her!"

o Our children are truly each other's best friends
- They even walk around in public with their arms linked together, joined at the hip!

☐ **Intellectual Formation: Doing Their Best in School is Their Duty**

o We let our children know that their education is the top priority.

o We encourage them to make the best use of the talents God has given them.

o This means taking school seriously.
- We limit extracurricular activities like sports.
- When these are engaged in to a disordered degree, they do tremendous damage to family unity.

- The soccer or baseball coach is not The Way, The Truth, and The Life.
- Baseball or dance is not the living bread that came down from heaven
- Christ did not say that whoever excels in a variety of sports will be raised on the last day.
- We are not saying that these things are not good in moderation, but we need to examine our priorities
  - Don't let the children and their activities run the family around by the nose.
    - Rather, do things together as a complete family unit.
    - A family has to spend time together.
  - There are no things we can give our children to make up for the time we should be spending with them
    - Find a place and a time to just be together often
  - Give our kids the time to be kids!
    - Let them use their minds and their imaginations
    - Let them enjoy the great outdoors
    - Let them read good books, our kids are avid readers. We take out 30-40 library books at a time.
    - In the summertime, our children create and perform plays for each other and the neighboring families, just like something out of Little Women

☐ **Apostolic: Give of yourself and God will reward you!**
  - To a sacrificial degree, it needs to hurt
  - In our family, the younger siblings are the older siblings' apostolate
    - We call them charges and chargemasters

- A big one is paired up with a little one, to help take care of their needs and work with them on
- Household jobs, training their replacement
- When a charge is trained in a job, he or she inherits that job from the chargemaster
- There are plenty of chores and responsibilities, starting as toddlers
- This teaches them that they are here not to be served, but to serve, as Christ taught us.
- It builds strong sibling bonds , they are major influences on each other's lives as they grow up

o You create good role models for your children to imitate, each other!

o Don't be afraid to demand sacrifice and responsibility from our children
  - It's a requirement of our baptismal call.
  - To bring others to Him

o Our children are involved in many ministries – apostolic work – bringing Christ to others. For instance, our oldest daughter Shannon, volunteered last summer on a internship promoting the prolife movie, Bella. Our daughter Tara gave a year after high school as a Catholic volunteer working with youth in Ireland. Our third daughter Grace, is part of the prolife club at AMU and regularly prays with other college students at local abortion clinics in Florida. Our daughter Colleen has volunteered as a Catholic missionary after high school. Deirdre, age 16 is involved in leading Catholic youth groups and in teaching religious education to children while in high school. Our 15 year old Bridget also leads a

Catholic girls club for 8th grade girls. She is a also involved in a weekly Christian Life group with teens her own age. Our son Shane, age 13, attends a minor high school seminary and is open to seeing if he is called to the priesthood. Our other 4 younger children are involved as members in Catholic youth clubs.

- o These are opportunities for our children to be engaged in changing society without being formed by the world.

☐ But, we as their parents, need to set the example of apostleship for our children
- o We need to lead by example.
- o Let our children see us fully engaged in giving ourselves to others, even outside our homes.
- o Our own family may be most important to us, but this does not relieve us of the responsibility of spreading the Kingdom of Christ to others, by getting involved in our parish, with evangelization and faith formation, to live out our baptismal call.

My Proverbs:

1. Never demand before motivating
Love is KEY!! Tell them and show them.
Love equals time: quality, listening, sitting with them
Talk and listen to them a lot
Know, love, accept them, and help each child better themselves.
Know them; what type of intelligence they have, will power, etc.
Temperament plays a part
To better help them find out what are their motivations/desires
What do they respond to; what is their love language
Do they respond to human things/spiritual things

Always positive, supernatural, spiritual; young people respond to the truth, ideals
We are their number one formators

2. Help them build solid convictions that'll last a lifetime

Now is the time, not later. We have them only for a short time, when they are young and formable.

Motivate your children a lot, so that they move themselves – so they learn to be self-motivated
Help them form convictions that will last once they leave home
Transcendent, long-term
Give them the faith now, live a sacramental life, so they will make their faith their own once they leave the house and go on to college, married life

All that really matters in life is doing God's will
That's the only thing that'll make you happy

Guide your children, stay with them; be an integral part of their life
Stay on top of what they are doing; be engaged in their lives

They will always need you
Don't be overprotective, but be there as a support

3. Be a parent, not a pal

Ok to say no
Set limits, etc.
I am their God-given authority
Always motivate out of love, not out of feelings, emotions, passions, etc.

Must establish true unity between the spouses
What did your dad say about that, you'll need to ask your dad, don't play each parent off the other
Be on the same page
Gives security and stability

With school, too, unity with what the school is trying to do
Always positive and unified
They want authority in their lives, they want order, not chaos; chaos creates a sense of loss of control, or meaninglessness, of instability

Discipline: external (room in order, etc.)
External order generates internal order
Orders our faculties: superior and inferior

Balance freedom and supervision
We like to keep them in a bubble but that might create rebellion
Must have prudent supervision (music, movies, internet)

4. Don't be afraid to let them suffer

Society says suffering is worst thing that can happen to them
Pope says: redemptive suffering makes us realize how much we need Christ
Teaches us Humility, reliance on God, we are not in control of our lives, He is.
Little sufferings strengthen us for bigger crosses as we grow

Responsibility at home, chores, teaches virtues of self-giving, selflessness, sharing, team work, etc. Teaches them generosity, that life isn't just about them.

Form their will power
Good to say no to oneself; teaches self-discipline and strengthens the will
Helps them to become men and women of character and conviction, of sacrificial love.

Pray a lot for guidance in our mission as wife and mother
For enlightenment on the truth and guidance in carrying it out consistently

First the Woman Then the Saint: Living a Life of Balance

Objectives:
- Setting priorities, creating a vocation statement
- Working to maintain balance
- How to make a flexible weekly and monthly schedule
- How to live that schedule

Resources:
- Holly Pierlot, *A Mother's Rule of Life* (Sophia Institute Press, 2004).
- James and Kathleen Littleton, *Better By the Dozen Plus Two* (Lulu Publishing Services, 2007).
- Franklin Covey, *Seven Habits of Highly Effective People* (Free Press, 1990).
- Franklin Covey Seminar, "What Matters Most" (Franklin Covey Productions).
- Vocation Statement from Spiritual Exercises Retreat Binder

In this talk, I am going to be completely open and honest with you, even to reveal to you one of the biggest sins I struggle with on a daily basis. Impatience!! Once someone asked me the question, what really aggravates me, and my immediate response was … wasting time!! My answer may reflect a sin I often struggle with which is impatience, but on the positive side, I like to think I'm working on the virtue of effectiveness! Efficaciousness and efficiency should be hallmarks of our vocation as apostles as well as unity and charity. But when we come down from the seemingly loftiness of the ideal, the realities of our everyday lives may cause us frustration! How can changing diapers, and dealing with the demands of raising a family truly lead us to heaven?? I have another secret to share with you. God has given us the means for our sanctification in the ordinary demands and responsibilities of our daily lives. What we are doing right now, where God has put us and through the very ordinary events and relationships with people in our state in life is our path to heaven!

Here is a quote from a homeschooling mother of five, but it could be from any one of us who has struggled with balancing our roles as wives, mothers and apostles, "Before my Rule, when all I could think about was how in the world I was ever going to get the house clean, I had no mental space for thinking of anything else. When I was constantly living my life based on my desires and whims (and needs) of the moment, I had no room in my heart for God. There were always more than enough things to fill my affections and my attention. A home and a life in disorder leads to 'dissipation' – a scattering of our interior faculties – and prevents us from becoming still enough to listen to God speaking inside us (Pierlot, *A Mother's Rule of Life*).

The heart of the "Rule," of our purpose here on earth, is contemplation, to unite our wills to God's will in order to become holy and bring others to heaven. Living in harmony, in balance with what God created us for, is our goal. But if we can't figure this out because our lives are so busy and unbalanced, and we don't know what we are indeed created for, how can we become holy? We need order (exterior order creates interior order) so we can hear and respond to God. This is part of what John the Baptist's call to us to "level the mountains of cares and anxieties, to fill in the valleys of busyness and details, and to make a straight path for the Lord" (see Matt. 3:3).

How? How do we create order and balance?

Step 1: Setting priorities: writing your vocation statement

What Is It?

Since Christ calls each soul from within a particular state in life and concrete daily circumstances to grow His kingdom, it is essential to personalize the spiritual commitments that will help us grow closer to Him so we come to know Him so we can share Him with others, so as to have a clear and motivating picture of who it is Christ is calling them personally to be. A tool to help determine this is a vocation statement.

Why Do It?

1. **Motivation**: Having a clear vision of the person Christ is calling me personally to become, and having

this written simply and clearly so I can glance at it each day, is a tremendous benefit during periods of dryness in prayer or the long, dark days of winter when we can find ourselves asking, "Why am I doing this, anyway?" The vocation statement is not a "to-do list," but a simple description of who I am called to be that motivates me to give my all out of love for Christ each day.

2. **Balance**: Because of the fast pace of life today, it seems Christians struggle as much as anyone else with becoming healthy and balanced persons while juggling many priorities. The vocation statement helps me to list the essential roles God has called me to fulfill: the things He will ask me about on the Last Day. If I find that I neglect one or more of these roles, I know I need to correct myself in order to achieve balance. At the same time, a vocation statement can help me let go of less important things when they conflict with my essential vocation.

3. **Focus:** There are so many attractive virtues and qualities of Christ to imitate that sometimes we make the mistake of trying "a little of this, a little of that." Having a clear picture of who Christ is calling me to be helps me to focus, making it a truly powerful instrument for my growth in holiness.

Another way to view your vocation statement is in the form of the 5 "Ps." In Holly Pierlot's book *A Mother's Rule of Life* subtitled *How to Bring Order to Your Home and Peace to Your Soul,* she outlines the 5 Ps which are the source for her (and our) vocation statements: Prayer, Person, Partner, Parent, Provider. These form the basis of her "Rule" of life as a homeschooling mother of five children. Another way to look at it is by means of living your life according to a "hierarchy of values" as referred to frequently in the book I authored with my husband, *Better by the Dozen Plus Two* subtitled *Anecdotes and a Philosophy of Life from a Family of Sixteen,* in which we list the order of priorities as God first, then spouse, family, then work/apostolate. And in doing so, we often have to take the narrow path, to be in the world, but not of it, to be counter-cultural, to make hard decisions that are in line with our priorities – in other words, to live authentically!

How Do I Create One?

In a climate of reflective silence and prayer, reflect on what God has created you for, those things by which He will judge you. This is not the time to worry about your shortcomings or sins; focus only what God is asking you to do, and the spirit He is asking you to bring to those roles. Dream a little! Since no one needs to see this but you and your spiritual director, describe the person that deep down you know you are called to be, and deeply want to be. This brief description will become something like a compass for your spiritual life, because you can use it to evaluate your priorities, goals, projects and progress.

Going back to the idea of balance, think of the roles you are called to fulfill in your life as the legs of a stool. As long as the legs stay in balance, the stool will be sturdy. You should include at least the following categories:

- As a baptized child of God
- As a married person
- [If applicable] As a parent
- As an apostle

Sample:

1) As a baptized person, I am called to have a deep, personal, passionate and faithful love for Jesus, nurtured in daily prayer, sacramental life, the life of grace and availability to souls through apostolate. I must constantly strive to make everything I do a function of a deep experience of Jesus' love for me. I am called to prioritize love, rather than letting my acts of piety and apostolate subtly become a "to-do" list that I accomplish on the strength of my own will.

2) As a wife, I am called to be God's instrument in showing my husband how much Jesus loves him. Whatever pressures internal and external weigh on

him, he must find in me a person who sees him as God sees him and believes in him even when he doesn't believe much in himself.

3) As a mother, I am the image my children will have of the Blessed Mother, and that reality must color my interactions with them. My fundamental goals with them are to help them discover Christ as their best friend; help them develop the human virtues that will serve as the platform for their true liberty -especially upright conscience, responsibility, firm will, maturity appropriate for their ages and capacity for sacrifice; to love and believe in them even they are making themselves and everyone around them miserable; to pray and sacrifice for them; to help them discover God's mission for their lives and never to interfere with it.

4) As an apostle, because I am a baptized Catholic I am called to respond to the needs of the Mystical Body of Christ and never be indifferent to them. Faith is the greatest gift that I can give to anyone, and I am called therefore to help the souls God puts in my path to discover Christ little by little. My vocation must touch and transform every aspect of my life, so that I can be an integrated, whole person and not a divided, compartmentalized one. Therefore, I will carry out my vocation as a wife, mother and apostle to the best of my ability while setting an example of a true Christian through detailed obedience to God's law in all I do and a right ordering of my priorities and use of time.

Step 2: Working to Maintain Balance: Living your life according to your Priorities - What Matters Most

Understanding Time Management: The Pyramid of Effectiveness and the Time Matrix

The Pyramid of Effectiveness:

The basic element of time is an event. The key to managing time is managing events well. The ability to manage events well leads to greater efficiency and effectiveness in our lives for Christ. The concepts provided in a Franklin Covey What Matters Most Seminar can be used to illustrate how the values and priorities laid forth in one's Vocation Statement.

Take a paper and pen and draw a large pyramid in your notes, with the larger end of the triangle being at the base.

- ☐ On Bottom (Base) list "What Matters Most" to you
  - o Your Governing Values (your highest priorities)
    - ▪ Your spiritual life
    - ▪ Your spouse
    - ▪ Your family
    - ▪ Your apostolate
  - o Your Roles (your key relationships and responsibilities) from your vocation statement
    - ▪ Wife
    - ▪ Mother
    - ▪ Apostle
  - o Your Mission (your unique purpose)
    - ▪ As Baptized Catholics it is to achieve heaven and lead others to Christ

- ☐ In Middle: Plan (how you will fulfill your mission by concrete means through long-term and weekly planning):
  - o The essential tool is a Planner (an agenda or daily calendar)
    - ▪ Planner Basics: prioritize and track tasks, capture and retrieve info
    - ▪ Planning: creates freedom by saving time

Let me share with you another secret. The secret to achieving balance is by balance is by living 100% in the moment. Managing your time *frees* you to be in the moment, to give yourself fully to the moment and to the people at hand, not worrying about what you have to do an hour from now or tomorrow because you have planned the time for that!!

The Time Matrix:

"Poor planning on your part is not a crisis on my part." This is a direct quote from my husband. What he means is that when I don't plan ahead, and things get out of control, the crisis arising from the chaos was created by my lack of planning and could have been prevented. And he also means that he is not responsible for fixing the mess that my lack of planning created. In other words, urgencies are not priorities; they act on priorities, creating stress.

The most urgent task is not always the most important! Most importantly, he is telling me that to refuse to be managed by crisis is to be a good leader, in the home and in the workplace.

To illustrate, the Franklin Covey Time Management Seminar uses the Time Matrix. Draw a large square on your paper and divide it into four squares. These are quadrants. To be an effective person and to manage time well, you'll want to spend most of your time in Quadrant 1 and 2, and mostly in Quadrant 2. You'll understand when you see what goes into each quadrant.

Quadrant 1: Important/Urgent Tasks - The Quadrant of Necessity
  - Examples of tasks: child care, feeding family, some work deadlines, pressing problems, deadline driven projects, meetings

Quadrant 2: Important/Not Urgent Tasks - The Quadrant of Leadership
  - Examples of tasks: prayer, apostolate responsibilities, exercise, nurturing friendships, nurturing family, preparation, prevention, planning

Quadrant 3: Not Important/Urgent - Quadrant of Deception
  - Examples of tasks: some phone calls, some work deadlines, housework that is not done so that becomes an emergency, many popular activities

Quadrant 4: Not Important/Not Urgent - Quadrant of Default
- Examples of tasks: most TV, busy housework, some shopping, gossip, time wasters, activities to excess

At the Top of the Pyramid of Effectiveness is action. Act by planning your time so that you spend most of it doing activities in Quadrant 2. For example, make a list of what you do every day. Keep this log for one week. Then look at how you spent your time. This exercise will show you where are your priorities, that is what you spend your time doing. Are you fulfilling your mission? Are these tasks helping you and souls get to heaven? If not, you need to adjust the amount of time you spend on that activity. Is it really one of your priorities? If not, then drop it!

Here are some tips to be more effective with your time:
- Prioritize your time with a planner
- Don't rely on your memory
- Eliminate floating paper!
- Use just one calendar for everything in your life!
- Schedule in your priorities first: Faith, Family, Apostolate
  - then the lesser important tasks and obligations will fit in around them
  - Put in your spiritual practices first!
    - Daily, weekly, monthly, yearly
  - Your children's school activities
  - Dates with individual children (one on one time)
  - Date night with your husband (at least one time a month!)
  - Your other commitments
    - extended family, professionally, socially
- Then every day in your planner, list what you need to do and prioritize the list
  - critical, must get done today
  - should get done today (use these the most)
  - could get done, but doesn't have to ... then plan it forward to another day
  - Then you place a number next to each letter in the order you'll do it

o   At the end of the day, be sure all your items are checked of or planned forward

Every Sunday evening do a weekly plan of your tasks, obligations and events for the week. You can ever add in a meal plan and grocery list ... be sure to plan in shopping and cooking time!

Here are ways you can also use your time effectively in handling mail:

- ☐ open it over your garbage can:
- ☐ Use the one touch rule
    - o   if it's important, take care of it now
    - o   If it is junk mail throw it out
    - o   If it can wait, use an In and Out Box
    - o   Go through it one time a week, schedule it!

You can also use the telephone more efficiently:

- o   Be courteous of the other person's time
- o   Use speed dial
- o   Use time in the car to make calls on cell phone
- o   Use an egg timer when on a phone call and watch your time!
- o   Use exit phrases
    - o   I'll just take a few moments of your time ...
    - o   I'll let you go now
    - o   For business calls, prepare ahead with an outline what you need to discuss
    - o   Invest in a headset so you can use your hands on another task while talking on the phone
    - o   Cordless and cell phones open up great possibilities!

You can use e-mail more efficiently by seeing it as a post office, not a social gathering!

- ▪   Open it only once in the morning and once at night
- ▪   Reply only to the ones you need to reply to
- ▪   Delete the rest

To be more efficient with your time, work free of clutter.

- Put away, give away or throw away
- A place for everything and everything in its place
- Files, file folders, file boxes, even for each of your children!
- Give yourself elbow room
- What is your greatest challenge within your workspace?
  - Get rid of the stuff on top of surfaces
  - Put the resources you refer to frequently within arm's reach
  - Only put out what you are currently working on
  - Do work in your quality time as it minimizes mistakes

To be more efficient with your time, use time spent waiting

- Take work with you in the car, spiritual reading, etc.
- Drop those futile useless activities
- Don't be afraid to say no, always give yourself time to pray
- First ask yourself if this task would make God happy?
- Is it the most effective use of your time, or can someone else do it?
- Will it help you fulfill the mission God has entrusted to you uniquely?

To be more efficient with your time, do the things that are the hardest first.

- get them over with!
- break big tasks into bite size pieces
- Put a time goal on each project
- Anybody can stand doing anything for 15 minutes!
- Then plan to do another 15 minutes on it later until it's done!

To be more efficient with your time, create more time!

- o Getting up earlier creates extra valuable time for what matters most like morning prayer and daily mass
- o Delegate
    - o Give jobs to others who can do it instead of you (even to your children.
    - o It is great on the job training and build character)
    - o Create a family system of chore division and rewards
    - o Let them do the same job until they are good at it.
    - o Then they train a younger sibling and work together on it for a period of time.
    - o Then they are rewarded by turning the job over to that child
    - o Then they move on to a different job, and so on!

Be more efficient with your time by avoiding distracting noise (radio, tv)

- o Quiet encourages prayer, even as you go about your daily tasks offering them to the Lord
- o You'll find you can concentrate better without noise and get the tasks done sooner and better.

Be more efficient with your time by planning for the unexpected.

- o Carpe Diem - seize the day (never put off to tomorrow what you can do today)
- o Free yourself for those unforeseen emergencies that tomorrow may bring like the sick child, the health crisis of a parent, the neighbor that needs a helping hand

Lastly, don't be so rigid in your scheduling that you don't have time to smell the roses or give your child a hug, your husband a sign of your love, your friend a smile, the stranger a kind gesture, and gratitude to God in spontaneous prayer.

In conclusion, invest in a planner! Get an audio tape on the Franklin system of time management and use a system of time management. By organizing your time you will

- o   Reduce stress
- o   Create more quality time
- o   Reach your goals
- o   Bring order to your home and
- o   Peace to your soul
- o   Be more effective for Christ
- o   Fulfill your unique mission on earth.

Prayer: How and Why to Do It
Explain goals of the talk
- To motivate you to make prayer a daily commitment
- To provide practical advice for praying a daily meditation

The Need for Prayer

Within the USA, we are everyday witnesses to moral decadence, or better said, to a crisis in our nation's moral conscience. We live in a society where God is pushed off to the sidelines, and this is done because those who are pushing God away are convinced this helps us to be freer. Pope John Paul II said that the essential crisis of contemporary man was his false understanding of freedom: he wants to be free to do any and everything, with no regard for cost or consequence. (See Pope John Paul II, *Redemptor Hominis,* 1979).

So we have a society accustomed to divorce, adultery, premarital relations, greed, consumerism, materialism; and therefore, we have a society of men and women who are selfish, insecure, and unable to give themselves and sacrifice themselves for others. Entirely self-focused, we do not have the stomach to hold convictions, and much less, fight for them. If we can do whatever we want in the pursuit of happiness, so can everyone else, so abortion and gay rights are ok.

It was recently reported in the National Catholic Register (Oct 25, 2006) that according to Nielsen Media Research, the average American home now has more television sets than people.. According to the researchers, there are 2.73 TV sets in the typical home and 2.55 people. Half of American homes have 3 or more TVs. Only 19% have just one. The research also showed that in the average home, a television set is turned on for more than a third of the day – 8 hours and 14 minutes. The average person watches four hours, 35 minutes of television each day.

A few more statistics to state the case for the need for prayer: The Roman Catholic Church in the United States is the nation's largest, most complex religious community. Its 61.5 million members live in almost twenty thousand parishes, located in every imaginable sub-division of America: in rich neighborhoods, poor neighborhoods, and middle-class neighborhoods; they are served by more than four hundred bishops and over forty-seven thousand priests. Roman Catholic "religious professionals" also include some eighty-five thousand sisters, six thousand brothers, and four thousand five hundred seminarians; twelve thousand permanent deacons.

In 1997, over a million infants were baptized into the Catholic Church, as were some seventy-three thousand adults; another eighty-eight thousand men and women, already baptized in other Christian communities, were received into full communion with the Catholic Church.

Almost nine hundred thousand Catholics made their first communion in 1997, more than six hundred thousand were confirmed, and some three hundred thousand couples solemnized their marriages in the Church.

The Catholic Church in the United States maintains six hundred hospitals, serving over sixty-five million patients annually, a large network of social service agencies (which assisted some eighteen million persons in 1997), and the world's largest independent educational system (with 240 colleges and universities, 1,347 high schools, and 7,151 elementary schools). More Catholics serve in the Congress of the United States than members of any other single denomination; a considerable percentage of the officer corps of the armed services are Roman Catholics.

Another statistic, this one a guess: some ten million Catholics go to Mass every Sunday in the USA; many have gone every Sunday of their lives.

These "statistics" prove something: being a Catholic, even going to mass, may mean nothing. Nothing?! If 60 million Americans know and love God, wouldn't they have a gargantuan impact on the life of the nation? Do we?

Am I preaching heresy, that the Mass is useless, or baptism, or confession? No. The sacraments certainly work their power by the very fact that they are validly celebrated, but the point is that the sacraments are powerless to effect change if the individual doesn't know and love God.

The Church professes the mystery of her faith in God in the Apostles' Creed, she celebrates that mystery in the sacraments, but that profession and celebration of faith need to be lived in a real, personal, even passionate relationship with the living God. That living relationship is developed only through prayer.

What Is Prayer?

St. John Damascene's classic definition: "Prayer is raising one's mind and heart to God, or requesting good things from God" (St. John Damascene, *Defide orth.* 3, 24:PG 94,1089C).

St. Therese of Lisieux's definition is also well-known: "Prayer is a surge of the heart; it is a simple look turned toward heaven, it is a cry of recognition and love, embracing both trial and joy" (St. Therese of Lisieux, *Manuscrits autobiographiques*, C 25r).

Prayer is man's communication with God, the place where the two meet. This may sound simplistic. It sounds too easy, too natural and we know from experience that we struggle with prayer in actuality. But it should be easy and natural! So let's stop for a second and look at how God made man "wired" for prayer.

Man is made in God's image. He is crowned with "glory and honor", stamped with God's likeness through his intellect and will (See Hebrews 2:7; Genesis 1:27). This is true, because it's part of Revelation: God made man in his own image and likeness, Genesis says (Genesis 1:27). Not only that, but God was in the habit of chatting with man "in the cool of the afternoon" which was the normal way people of the ancient near East spent time with their friends (see Genesis 3:8-13). So the message from Scripture is that God was very close and friendly with man. When he sinned, man lost the easy intimacy of his union with God, but he is nevertheless called to it all the same.

God calls man first. God stretches out his hand first. Man may forget God, may run from him, may set up his own priorities or idols, but God calls him to that mysterious encounter called prayer. "Within man's heart is a space that cannot be filled up except by God," said Blaise Pascal (See Blaise Pascal, Pensees, trans. A. J. Krailsheimer, London: Penguin, 1993, 45).

So then, prayer is simply a conversation with God, a child speaking humbly with her father, a daughter speaking with her dad. It is one on one time with Jesus. This means we need to develop a personal relationship with Jesus Christ. The best possible way to meet Jesus, to come to know him is through daily meditation because it is truly a very personal conversation with Him.

Fallacies You May Be Thinking

I will pray, do my meditation when I am holier. No! St. Teresa of Avila compared praying to watering our garden from which would flower virtues and thus holiness. She also compared mental prayer to a door through which graces flow into our lives which enable us to become holy. (See St. Teresa of Avila, *The Way of Perfection*, C 22).

We don't become holy and then start praying. We begin and persevere in prayer in order to acquire virtues and then become holy. Virtue and holiness are the fruit of prayer!

Types of Prayer

Vocal prayer consists in reciting ready-made prayers, either silently or aloud, uniting the intention of your heart to the meaning of the words. Examples of vocal prayers are novenas, the Our Father, the Rosary and even the Mass. All Christians should have their favorite vocal prayers, the ones that resonate best with their own experience of Christ, the ones they can go back to in moments of dryness, sickness, or difficulty.

Meditation is less formal than vocal, recitation of ready-made prayers. The beautiful thing is that meditation will even enrich your experience of vocal prayers. They will not become routine and ritualistic, will not become stale, if you are faithful to your daily meditation, ever developing and deepening your personal relationship with Jesus Christ!

Meditation consists in lifting the hard and mind to God through focused reflection on some truth of God's revelation. It involves the intellect, the imagination, the memory, and the emotions – the whole person.

In meditation, as you turn your gaze to God's self-revelation in Christ, you are moved to respond to what you discover there, and you converse with God in the silence of your own heart, using words that flow naturally from your reflection.

The best source for your daily meditation is the gospels. What better way to come to know, love and imitate Christ? Other sources to use can be good Catholic works like Imitation of Christ, Imitation of Mary, the Lives of the Saints, etc.

One caveat regarding meditation versus spiritual reading - it is not meditation unless you are stopping periodically in your reading and conversing with God about what you are reading. Spiritual reading is for the intellect – meditation is for the heart!

Contemplation consists of a more passive (and more sublime) experience of God. If mediation is the soul's inspired quest to discover God, contemplation is God's lifting of the soul into himself, so that it effortlessly basks in the divine light. It is the soul's silent gazing upon the grandeur of God.

How to Do a Daily Meditation

Start with the Come, Holy Spirit prayer, then the preparatory acts of Faith, Hope, and Love; of gratitude and humility. Read your passage, then reflect on it:

- Begin with the scene: What do you see? Who are the characters? What are they saying? What are they doing? Use your imagination and memory. Try to imagine the Gospel scene – with all of its sights, sounds, scenery, smells, etc.

- If the meditation is to be practical, we need to ask what does Our Lord want us to learn from this scene. Identify the virtue or vice. How is it being manifested? What is God saying to me personally here?
- Why do I want this virtue? What does Our Lord say about it and the necessity of having this virtue? How does it relate to the duties in my state of life? How can acquiring this virtue or eliminating this vice help me as a wife, a mom, a student, a co-worker?
- How can I get this virtue? If I am failing in this virtue, where do I fail, how do I feel? Get specific so that you can make a concrete resolution. (Charity - I resolve that today, at such-and-such a time, in such-and-such a place, when I am tempted to do such-and-such, I will pray and do the opposite.)
- Conclusion: Lord, what is the next step? What do you want me to do? Form a resolution which can simply be an attitude or disposition that you want to live through the day based on the virtue you examined, and what you have determined God's will is for you as a result of doing this meditation. It needs to be personal and practical for you.

To summarize, it is a four step process: Concentrate, Consider, Converse, Commit. These four steps are taken from *The Better Part*, (Circle Press: 2007) by Father John Bartunek.

Conclusion: Don't Get Discouraged

- We get discouraged because we think we are wasting time - but that's exactly what the Devil wants you to think. The only failure you can have in the spiritual life is to stop trying, to give up.
- Baby steps: if you're a beginner at prayer, think of an infant learning to walk: first he needs bodily

coordination, then he learns to scoot, then crawl, he toddles, then walks, and in time he even begins to run.

- Practice makes perfect: just as you learn how to walk by walking, so you learn how to pray by praying. When you fall down, you get up. A simple way to characterize the saints is that we all fall, but saints get back up.

- Be perfect: in holiness (perseverance)... not perfectionism, meaning if the conditions aren't quite perfect, you don't feel well, you forgot to prepare, etc., then you don't pray. But pray anyway and trust that God will make it perfect.

- Bring your specific difficulties to a spiritual guide. How blessed you are if you are able to receive spiritual direction!

In closing, I'd like to leave you to reflect upon this prayer from Blessed Mother Teresa of Calcutta, entitled A Last Prayer:

A Last Prayer, by Mother Teresa of Calcutta

I worry that some of you still have not really met Jesus – one-to-one – you and Jesus alone.

We may spend time in chapel – but have you seen with the eyes of your soul how He looks at you with love?

Do you really know the living Jesus – not from books, but from being with Him in your heart? Have you heard the loving words He speaks to you?

Ask for the grace; He is longing to give it.

Until you can hear Jesus in the silence of your own heart, you will not be able to hear Him saying, "I thirst" in the hearts of the poor.

Never give up this daily intimate contact with Jesus as the real living person – not just the idea.

How can we last even one day without hearing Jesus say, "I love you?" Impossible. Our soul needs that as much as the body needs to breathe the air. If not, prayer is dead – meditation, only thinking.

Jesus wants you each to hear Him speaking in the silence of your heart.

Be careful of all that can block that personal contact with the living Jesus.

The devil may try to use the hurts of life, and sometimes our own mistakes – to make you feel it is impossible that Jesus really loves you, is really cleaving to you.

This is a danger for all of us. And so sad, because it is completely the opposite of what Jesus is really wanting, waiting to tell you.

Not only that He loves you, but even more – He thirsts for you.

He loves you always, even when you don't feel worthy. When not accepted by others, even by yourself sometimes – He is the one who always accepts you.

Only believe – you are precious to Him.

Bring all your suffering to His feet – only open your heart to be loved by Him as you are. He will do the rest.

Mother Teresa: 1910 – 1997

Becoming One with the Creator, (Not the Created): How to Practice Catholic Meditation

May 17, 2008

Prayer. What Is Prayer? Often when Christian's think of prayer, we seem to have in mind something that we must do, something we must become good at, as if it was all about our efforts, our techniques, our concentration, our abilities. We say, "if only I prayed more, if only I had time to pray, if only I knew how to pray." When seen in that way - that it is all about what we do or need to do or become better at doing, prayer can confuse us, discourage us. We tend to give up when we don't feel consolation, see any improvement, or our prayers don't seem to be answered.

This morning, I'm going to let you in on the secret to prayer. It's not about us, what we do. It's about what God does, how God looks at us. And what God is doing for us in prayer is nothing other than giving us God's very self in love.

God is total Love, total Gift. And prayer is what God does for us in our soul. It is God drawing us to Him in love. "For God so loved the world that he gave his only Son, so that everyone who believes in him might not perish but might have eternal life" (John 3:16). God's love for us is limitless, unconditional. And it is through Jesus Christ that God reveals His total, limitless unconditional love for us. We are simply asked to open ourselves, to empty ourselves, in order to receive this unconditional love.

For our part, what we have to do is allow ourselves to be loved, to be there for Love to love us.

How and when are we "there" for Love to love us? By receiving Christ in the Eucharist daily or as often as possible, by adoring and consoling Him in the Blessed Sacrament at a Holy Hour, by spending time with Him to listen and be with Him in quiet recollection, by making time each day to come to know him more through Scripture and the teachings of our Catholic faith in order to love him more ... by praying.

But prayer is not a matter of our finding some way of contacting God, of sending him some kind of a signal, of making God real to us, of getting hold of a secret key with which to open the mystic door. It's about *Faith* – real Faith. Not just a head knowledge, but a heart knowledge – a real knowing that God my Father loves me with an eternal love. And because I know this, I love God back. I respond to His love.

This realization, this conviction demands an equal response to that divine Love freely given to me by my Creator, who created me out of love for no reason but to love *me*! It calls for a freely given response in love to Love. It calls for a living of that knowledge, of a living out of that knowledge. It means that our way of looking at things, our actions, our attitudes arise from this motivation, this source, that God created us to love us, and we are created to love Him back! It's that simple.

So how do we do this? How do we love God back? How do we show Him our love? We do it by doing His will; by uniting our will to His will; by becoming one with Him; by surrendering ourselves to him; by removing all the obstacles in our hearts to loving Him; by putting our securities, our trust in God alone, in our Creator - not in His created things, not in ourselves, in our plans, in our abilities, and talents, in our methods, techniques and programs. We show our love for Him by becoming simple in our prayer, child-like and trusting; by letting ourselves be drawn by Him; by letting go, and letting God; by going to the source, to the living water, and letting ourselves drink of the water drawn for us by Him.

Therein lies the secret to prayer.

A Sample Daily Meditation: Basic Steps:
Choose a passage from the Bible so I can come to know, love and imitate Christ.
Focus on the virtue being lived therein and how I can obtain it in my life.

Use the 4 steps: Concentrate, Consider, Converse, Commit. These four steps are taken from *The Better Part*, Circle Press, 2007 by Father John Bartunek.

Concentrate:
Very Important: Looking for interior silence and presence of God, dispositions and motivations, putting aside distractions make preparatory acts of faith, hope, love; gratitude and humility. Be spontaneous, make it yours, and only use formulas if you feel very tired or distracted but be present in your prayer.

Constantly refresh this basic methodology of beginning your prayer. Enter into the presence of God. Desire a personal experience of God's transforming love, not necessarily a consoling experience, but rather an experience in Faith.

Start with the Come Holy Spirit Prayer
Make Spontaneous Acts of Faith, Hope, Love
Lord, I believe in you. Lord I hope in you. Lord, I love you.
Petition: I ask that through this meditation, I may have the grace to see myself clearly as God sees me and loves me.
Fruit: To let go of myself, to surrender, and let His love transform me.

Consider:
Slowly read your passage, then reflect on it.
The goal of the meditation is to go over the truths of the gospel, letting God penetrate your mind and heart more deeply with these truths in order to be more convinced and faithful.

Serenely you are looking for the insights that God wants to reveal to you for you to ponder.
Sometimes it is easy and other times very difficult to capture what God wants to say. Silence is key so He can allure you like that gentle breeze that moves your heart; maybe a text, or a thought, a spiritual intuition. That is where God is attracting you, to the spiritual sustenance you are in need of.

Remember, THE HOLY SPIRIT is in charge

Example from The Woman at the Well passage, John 4:5-42
The Samaritan woman has a life changing Encounter with Christ through prayer, communication with God and uniting her will to His, her interior life is transformed by Christ, and she is called to conversion and evangelization.

Begin with the scene:
What do you see? Who are the characters? What are they saying? What are they doing? Use your imagination and memory. Try to imagine the Gospel scene – with all of its sights, sounds, scenery, smells, etc.

Ancient town, surrounded by mountains and desert plains.

See Christ, tired, and weather beaten.

The Samaritan woman approaches – hottest part of the day, she is tired of life; human love has not satisfied her.

Absolute silence, routine, tedium, subtle self hate has worn down her enthusiasm for life.

Christ sees into her soul and loves her

What strikes me about this passage? What does this mean? What does it tell me about Christ, the Church, the meaning of life?

Christ had to pass through Samaria

The truth about the Love of Christ, the thirst of Christ. Not physical but spiritual thirst for souls

Make it personal:
What does it mean to me in my own life today? How is this truth relevant to my own reality, my struggles, my vocation as mother and wife. My need for Christ…

I am that woman – I identify with the Samaritan
Tired, worn down from the routine, weight of the responsibilities

Since my first deep encounter with Christ's love, my own enthusiasm has waned...

Christ waits for me at the well.

Just his gaze invites me to a higher love, higher ideal

Remembering my first experience of knowing Jesus as a person and true friend; how it transformed my interior and filled me with new joy.

How he looked for that opportunity; He waited for the perfect chance for a deep experience

Divine love changes me, heals me and cures me of my past. Brings me to new life in Him

Remain in silence:
Peace and union with God until you feel the need to go on.

Next:
If the meditation is to be practical, we need to ask what does Our Lord want us to learn from this scene. Identify the virtue – surrender, self knowledge leading to conversion and transformation through realization of God's great love for me personally that He wants to heal me, wants to love me. How is it being manifested? What does our Lord say and or do?

Give me a drink – What are you saying? You always take the initiative with my soul; you invite me to a deeper share in your Divine Life – Calling me to intimate friendship.

See the gaze of Christ: merciful, offering a love which is donation – He only wants to give – "Give me a drink " is Christ's conversation starter—you open the door of my heart

"IF you knew the Gift of God and who is asking you for a drink......"

You would give priority to me always and everything else will fall into place

Let go of the "7 loves...." To which your heart is attached....... Activism, to do list, vanities, excessive preoccupation for children's futures, finances or the security of material possessions, my plans for my future, etc.

The gift of God, is an invitation to a deep interior life. How can I develop this interior life? How can I go into His Heart – that well spring of Eternal Life?

Converse:
Why do I want this virtue of self-knowledge and surrender to God's will? What does Our Lord say about it and the necessity of having this virtue? How does it relate to the duties in my state of life? How can acquire this virtue to help me as a wife, a mom, a professional working woman, an apostle for Christ?

Christ asks me to develop the virtues of piety (a deeper prayer life) and is asking me like the Samaritan woman to be an apostle for Christ, to bring Him to souls and share the good news.
With that experience of Christ I have to "leave my water jar" and bring Him to everyone I meet.

Talking to Christ as my friend, "You want to give me the Living Water."

Please, Lord, give me the gift of prayer, the ability to turn to you in the middle of my daily duties and struggles. Give me the ability to go to the "well" to be with you, to stay centered on you, in the midst of my daily responsibilities.

Invoke Mary to help with my interior life – our model of a woman of faith.

Commit: (finishing words or dialogue)
- How can I get this virtue? If I am failing in this virtue, where do I fail, how do I feel? Get specific so that you can make a concrete resolution. Think about when I

fail, what triggers it, what circumstances trigger me to rely more on myself and less on God?

- Lord, what is the next step? What do you want me to do? Form a resolution which can simply be an attitude or disposition that you want to live through the day based on the virtue you examined, and what you have determined God's will is for you as a result of doing this meditation. It needs to be personal and practical for you.
- Make a resolution: Check it at in your examination of conscience, balance of the day before bedtime.
- Example: I resolve to let go of my worries, preoccupations, and plans for myself today and what I will do to obtain them with my own abilities, but rather I will surrender and let God use me as his instrument. I will be attentive to the inspirations of the Holy Spirit and act on what He wants me to do. I will empty myself of myself to listen to Him within me and to act on his inspirations.

Ask our Lady to help me be faithful to my resolution

The best conclusion to every prayer is "Yes" to Christ! Keep following Him, keep growing in love, keep fighting to be faithful to his will.

Conclusion:
We give you thanks Almighty God for all your benefits. You who live and reign forever and ever. Amen.

Spiritual Direction: The Whys and Hows (An Outline for a Talk)

Clarification of Terms:

Spiritual Direction refers to spiritual direction given by a priest (spiritual director)
Spiritual Guidance refers to spiritual direction given by the laity (spiritual guide)
Spiritual Guidee is the one seeking guidance or direction

The Nature of Spiritual Direction:

An educational endeavor
To help a soul grow morally, spiritually and apostolically (in service to others)
Over time to help the soul reach spiritual perfection
From the spiritual guide's perspective:
Our Goal with the Holy Spirit:
  o To bring you to a much deeper moral depth (what you do)
  o And spiritual depth (what you believe)
  o How that inner part is going to be expressed on the outside
The Spiritual Guide is never going to be satisfied with your mediocrity … nor will Christ
The Spiritual Guide see souls like Christ sees them
When Christ looks at you He sees all the good first
Then secondly your frailities and weaknesses
The Spiritual Guide wants the best for you
The Spiritual Guide seeks your good and wants you to excel
The Spiritual Guide is there to help make you holy
To bring you to perfection.

What Spiritual Guidance Is:

A definition: a dialogue of faith in the Church between two persons who seek to know the will of God in one's daily reality concretely.

Three players; The guide, the guidee, and the Holy Spirit

A dialogue in faith:
Must have a supernatural atmosphere
It's an atmosphere of faith
That's the air we breath
Without faith, it's not spiritual guidance … its advice.
Faith is what it's all about
If we don't have faith, we can't have hope and we can't love.

In the Church:
It's Catholic
The vocabulary, the concepts of sound doctrine of the Catholic Church

What Spiritual Guidance is Not:

A friendly conversation on spiritual things
Not clinical therapy, you'll have to go to a psychiatrist for that
Not an unloading session
It's about your spiritual life … a growing real and personal relationship with Christ which will affect how you live your life!
Problems/difficulties can be brought up at the very end of the session (special circumstances affecting their peace, either positively or negatively)
Spiritual Guidance focuses on working on the positive – what has been accomplished first, where the soul is going - on a goal
Not just advice
It's guidance, not spiritual suggestion
You have to apply the medicine or you won't grow
You'll be back saying the same thing a year from now

The first year of your spiritual guidance is one of very basic formation
Prepares you well
Program of Life the first several sessions
How to do a meditation
Law of graduality in living their spiritual commitments
Slowly incorporating more and more
Regular spiritual guidance is essential as is:

Self-Formation in the Catholic Faith:

Let it suffice to say that the task of formation in the faith is impossible if one doesn't have the self-motivation to do it, from within
One's formation has much to do with one's personal conviction
That we have to act and be what we are regardless ... this is authenticity
Entails internalizing our vocation, our state in life and living our spiritual commitments whether you are being watched or not, until they become part of your life
There must be the desire to reach the ideal that Christ wants of us.
One needs to take it as one's own responsibility
This is what the spiritual guidee needs to do
Spiritual guidance helps to form this self-conviction in us
The benefits of spiritual guidance is it increases our humility simply because of the act of opening ourselves and admitting our weaknesses and faults and it offers us practical guidance in the light of the Holy Spirit.

The How Tos:

Before: pray and reflect – throughout the whole month prepare for your next appointment and pray for your guide. Be concrete, write lights down, and things you might be struggling with. Don't wing it when you get there.

Make the appointment.

Go. Show up. Make it a priority. Be humble. Be honest. Don't try to impress your guide. In reality you are working with the Holy Spirit and he knows you intimately already.

During: Be open. Come with an attitude of openness, and listen carefully. Be trusting, and be prepared to be flexible, letting the Holy Spirit take over the direction of your time with your guide. Let the inspirations and insights the freedom to be brought forth. Be prepared to receive constructive criticism with a humble heart.

Often what you hear you need to work on is what you already know you need to do. Don't be seeking anything unusual.

After: Just Do it. Spiritual direction is effective to the extent that you put into practice what you learn. Don't compare yourself with others either and what they might be directed to practice. Your path to holiness is unique to you. Make a resolution to work on during the time between your appointments. Commit to this and reflect on it during the month, evaluating your growth in that virtue or action.

Conclusion: Be patient with yourself. Our whole lives are the time we work out our salvation here on earth, and our eternity in heaven.

What is Love? Total Self-Giving – A Workshop

Format of Workshop:
Welcome and Introductions
What is Love?? Seek spontaneous answers from group.
Opening Prayer (Come Holy Spirit, Our Father, Hail Mary)
Directed Meditation (Gospel Reflection)
Personal Questionnaire - Silent Prayer before Christ in Tabernacle
Conference Talk – examples of self-giving love from our book (motherhood)
Case Studies in Small Groups – with resolutions
Cases of People Living Sacrificial Self-Giving love through Service to Others
- Pope JPII - servant of the servants
- Blessed Mother Theresa of Calcutta – "I have found the paradox that if I love until it hurts, then there is no hurt, but only more love."
- Blessed Mother – her humility – I am the humble servant of the Lord, her self-giving YES
- People today in the news, people in our own lives (priests, family members, our own mothers, our husbands, other husbands, women we know, etc.
- Sharing of case study – resolutions

Conclusion - What is Love??? Seek new spontaneous answers.
Love is Total Self-Giving
Closing Prayer

Directed Meditation (Gospel Reflection on Mark 12:28-37)
What does Christ tell us is the most important commandment?

Point 1: Love God and Love our Neighbor - Jesus links forever the commandment to love God with the commandment to love one's neighbor as oneself. If all we did in our spiritual lives were to strive to our utmost to fulfill these commandments, we would very soon be saints.

How much must we love? What is love?

Point 2: Love is total self-giving – True Love Is Generous (Mark 12:1-11)

Personal Questionnaire before Blessed Sacrament
(Bow before the altar, genuflect before the tabernacle)
Christ truly present – Body, Blood Soul and Divinity – waiting here for all time
His total donation of self so that we may enter into the gates of heaven …

Let us take full advantage of being in his presence to receive his Love, so we can give it back to others, to our families, to coworkers … to become like him.

1. Do I really feel that God loves me? Can I reflect on an experience of God's personal love and mercy.
2. When I think about the incarnation, passion and death of Christ, am I moved to respond in love and gratitude?
3. How have I responded to God's love for me in my life? Have I been generous in my response, in my self-giving love to God and to others in my life? What concrete acts of love have I performed out of love for God toward my neighbor?

Conference Talk
Chapter 1 of the author's book *Better by the Dozen Plus Two*, by James and Kathleen Littleton summarize how we came to be family (read bottom pg 15-16)
Chapter 5 On Motherhood (read page 71-74, then78-79)

Case Study
Cases of People Living Sacrificial Self-Giving love through Service to Others
• Pope JPII - servant of the servants
• Mother Theresa - Blessed Mother Theresa of Calcutta, "I have found the paradox that if I love until it hurts, then there is no hurt, but only more love."
• Blessed Mother – her humility, the humble servant of the Lord, her self-giving "yes".

• People today in the news, people in our own lives (priests, family members, our own mothers, our husbands, other husbands, women we know, etc.)

Discuss Causes – why do they do what they do
Discusses Consequences – the repercussions on themselves, on others for what they do
Share any lights, inspirations to live this in our own lives
Come up with a personal resolution – how we can live love (generous self-giving in service to others) in our lives, how we can respond to God's love for us in practical ways to our neighbor (husband, children, family, friends, coworkers)

Zeal For Souls: Living Our Baptismal Call

"I Thirst." These words were the ones Jesus spoke while hanging on the cross. They are also the words Mother Teresa heard when Jesus gave her the mission to serve the poorest of the poor. Christ's thirst was not just a bodily thirst for liquid, but a thirst for souls. When Mother Teresa heard these words, she dedicated her mission to help alleviate Christ thirst. Years after her call, she printed the words from Psalm 68:21 on a holy card, "I looked for one that would comfort me and I found none." She also wrote on that card, "Be the *one*."

As baptized Christians, we have a duty to bring Christ to everyone we meet. Christ thirsts for souls and we are the hands, feet and voice to bring those souls to Him. In Ephesians, Paul tells us that we all have different gifts and we are to use them together to bring Christ to others. As St. Paul wrote, "And he gave some as apostles, others as prophets, others as evangelists, others as pastors and teachers, to equip the holy ones for the work of ministry, for building up the body of Christ" (Ephesians 4:11-12). So, we are to work zealously for souls in a spirit of unity with the gifts and talents God has given us.

In a world so consumed with everything except God, how do we bring Christ to others? We can change the world by our prayer, example and working with a spirit of unity and charity putting God first through prayer and the sacraments to get closer to Christ, our program of life to help us live out a Christ-like life, and through our personal self-giving service to others to bring Christ to the world. The first two, our prayer and Christ-like example, are necessary in order to work effectively in service to others.

Why do we need to pray in order to bring Christ to others? In order to convince anyone of anything, we must be convinced ourselves. If we don't love Christ with our whole heart and soul and make Him our best friend, we will not convince others to go to Him. Thus, we need to pray and make him our best friend, otherwise, we will work half-heartedly, lack courage when the situation is tough and make excuses for ourselves. We will get caught up in the business of this life and end up putting God in the "spare time" category. I would like to use an example from the book, *He Leadeth Me*, by Father Walter Ciszek (Ignatius Press, 1995). Men in concentration work camps who did manual labor sixteen hours per day and had barely enough food rationed to them would skip meals when they heard of a secret Mass so that they would be able to receive Jesus in Holy Communion. Would we do that knowing we were already starving and had hours of hard labor ahead of us? These men knew in their hearts that Christ is the Eucharist and they lived this out.

Likewise, through prayer and the sacraments, we get closer to God by offering prayer throughout the day. If we truly pray, we will grow closer to Christ and He will become our best friend. We will begin to live our lives like the men in the concentration camp, by putting God above all else.

Once we put prayer first, God comes first and this is reflected in our example. How are we living our lives? Do we just "do" our prayer commitments, but live without charity? We all have our root defect and need to be vigilantly working on the virtues needed to counteract this. I am sure that we all have met the pious person who lacks charity, maybe speaks poorly of others or is angered by the noise of children at Church. How will that attitude bring others to Christ? Now even more than ever, in a world so consumed with sin, we need to be that shining example of Christ's love. I'll give two situations to highlight this point. A lady with several children goes to the store. She looks haggard, is wearing torn sweats and yells at the kids the whole time. Her kids have not have their needs met and are crying the whole time. Her example will most likely reaffirm someone else's opinion, that it is not good to have so many children. On the other hand, our example could lead to a different response. Let suppose that same woman with the five kids dresses herself well, feeds her kids and takes care of their needs and then goes shopping with them. She is happy and calmly, the whole family does the shopping. That same women who would have been reaffirmed for not having more children may see this wonderful group and think, "Wow, I guess you can have a lot of kids and make it work. Maybe I should have more children." Our example to the world is very important. That is why our program of life and spiritual guidance is necessary. We will be striving to attain virtues so we can be living a real Christian life filled with charity.

We cannot just stop our Christian living with our example. We need to do more and are called to do more. This is where service to others comes in. We must bring Christ to others by actively working to do so by lending a helping hand when someone is in need. But to give to others, you first need yourself to be totally committed to Christ. He must be your best friend. You would do anything for your best friend. Your best friend, Christ is thirsting for souls. He has brought you into this world, with all your talents and His gifts of faith hope and love, and is waiting for you to help Him change the world. You are his hands, his feet, his arms. If you are lacking motivation, if your life seems too busy, if you find you are making excuses not to serve Him, go to him in prayer. Make him your first priority again. It might mean restructuring your family life. Sometimes those extra-curricular activities get out of hand. You might need to scale back in order to make Christ first again, but it will be worth it. The reason we were put on this earth was to know, love and serve Christ and bring him to the world. We must constantly look at our lives and really evaluate if this is what we are doing. It is easy for life to spiral down that incredibly busy path, where we don't even have time to go to the bathroom. Don't let that happen. Pray first. Visualize him hanging on the cross, looking right at you. Meditate on him struggling for the air to breathe as he says, "I thirst." He is begging you for souls. So let's get out there and bring souls to Christ, so we may help that thirst. Then, we will be the disciples He has called us to be.

Littleton Family Manual

Updated Littleton Family House Rules and Program 9/5/2003

Do everything in prayer and charity.

When wake up pray morning prayers, make beds, and straighten rooms before coming down for breakfast.

Be up at 5:30am on school days to avoid rushing. Down for breakfast by 5:55am.
Breakfast done by 6:20am for fasting before daily Mass.

Have charges completely prepared to leave for school before you leave the house.

No playing in morning. Work on house straightening.

Patience, mercy, soothing encouraging speech. OBEDIENCE.

No one leaves kitchen until cleaning is done after meals.

Use time wisely to get homework done.

No movies at all during school week.

All clothes hung up or folded in drawers. Nothing on floors ever.

Shoes always hung up in garage.

After school no snacks. Do homework.

Dinner at 4:30pm. Clean up. Then night prayers right away. Can play for a time inside or out. Get little ones ready for bed. Then everyone does homework, and to bed.

Stay focused on work. Then there will be plenty of time to do everything without being rushed.

Remember to work as a team so work goes smoothly. How would a body work effectively if two arms decided to disobey the head and do things their own way in their own time?

I love you and need your help with this. I am counting on you, as is Christ. Do everything for love of Christ and souls.

Each weekend we will take a family vote to award the best three team players on the Littleton team.

Remember to encourage and build up. Don't be negative. Make the work fun by making little contests and such.

Love,

Dad

Saturday Jobs for Littletons 6/23/2004

Everyone cleans their rooms to perfection, and helps with laundry

Tara:
- Clean inside tubs and showers weekly
- Shine all stainless steel in house
- Clean all kitchen surfaces, wood table with Murphy Oil soap, and counters with Windex
- Dusting whole house
- Clean inside fridge and stove top
- Clean inside microwave
- Inspects entire house for orderliness and cleanliness
- Clean out Hyundai
- Pull weeds and general landscaping

Bridget:
- Wash bathroom floors and tile floors on basement stair landings
- Vacuum all rooms
- Tidy first floor and upstairs
- Clean vans
- Wash all bathroom surfaces and toilets, and floors around and behind toilets
- Clean bathroom mirrors
- Vacuum both basement stairways, and carpets in basement
- In charge of laundry
- Keep inside of Dad's car clean including dusting and carpets cleaned with wet rag

Shane:
- Sweep all hardwood floors with regular broom before mopping
- Mop all hard wood floors and into corners
- Sweep basement
- Keep basement organized and neat at all times, and checks under couches
- Sweep garage and keep organized at all times

Fiona:
- Mop all hard wood floors and into corners
- Use wet rag to wash under all counters in kitchen into corners
- Organize coat closet and garage at all times
- Clean basement
- Take out all garbage and replace bags
- Clean vans with Bridget
- Help Bridget to wash bathroom floors
- Help Bridget with vacuuming

Maura:
- Sweep kitchen
- Organize all desks and dressers in all children's rooms.
- Organize in all bathroom cabinets
- Organize and clean under all beds
- Organize all bathroom cabinets and drawers

Clare:
- Dust mop all hard wood floors
- Organize all closets n children's rooms
- Wash all wood work on stairway with Murphy Oil soap
- Wash all kitchen chairs with Murphy Oil Soap

Patrick and Mairead:
- Wash all kitchen chairs with Murphy Oil Soap
- Help clean their rooms
- Help bigger kids with jobs

Littleton Family Schedule After School and Evening 8/24/2006

Stay on schedule!

Do everything with a sense of sacrifice for love of Christ and souls.

Everyone is to do a minimum of one hour per night homework and study, whether they have homework or not! All homework is to be completed before going to sleep.

3:30pm: Picked up from school. Work on homework on way home in van.

4:00pm: Arrive home. Laundry and straighten house. No Snacks.

4:15pm: Prepare dinner and set table. Everyone helps.

4:30pm: Dinner.

4:50pm: Clean up. Work as team. See "Kitchen Jobs".

5:05pm: Pray.

5:25pm: Straighten house, play outside

5:45pm: Homework for those who have it, rest can play outside

6:45pm: Get ready for bed. Showers. Dry dishes. Straighten house.

7:00pm: To bedrooms. No talking or getting up. Go right to sleep. Finish homework if not done.

Littleton Family Morning School Day Program 7/26/09

(Lunches, breakfasts prepared and showers taken night before)

5:20am: Dad up

6:00am: Mom up

6:00am: Kids up.

6:15am: Morning prayers said, beds made, room clean by 6:15am.

6:30am: Get dressed, faces washed, teeth brushed, hair done by 6:30am.

6:30am: Down for breakfast

7:00am: Clean kitchen and prepare to leave.

7:20am: Everyone in car as we leave now for 7:45am Mass.

It is essential that we keep exactly on schedule to avoid disorder. Complaints are welcome, as those making these will be given extra work, which is always welcome.

Do everything with charity and love of Christ. Thank you for all your great work children. I love you.

Sincerely yours in Christ,

Dad

Kitchen Jobs for Littletons 7/26/09

Everyone clears table after meal

Everyone fully dressed with hair done and rooms neat and clean before meal.

No one leaves kitchen until all work done. Teamwork. Help others after your assigned work is done.

Work cheerfully, with attention to every detail of job until completely finished

Fiona:
- Sets table, plates, silverware, napkins
- Supervises kitchen work.
- Give wet rags to Clare, Patrick, Mairead, Brighde, Shealagh
- Washes Kitchen table
- Wash up babies
- Clean downstairs bathroom with spray
- Start Laundry
- Open blinds

Maura:
- Does dishes
- Clean inside microwave
- Clean inside fridge and stove top
- Inspect entire house for orderliness and cleanliness
- Clean children's bathroom with spray

Clare:
- Unload dishwasher before meal
- Pours drinks
- Wash all kitchen chairs
- Move chairs during mopping
- Clean all kitchen surfaces, and counters
- Shine all stainless steel in house with vinegar spray
- Laundry hampers down
- Clean big girls' bathroom with spray

Patrick:
- Laundry hampers down
- Sweep
- Mop kitchen hard wood floors and into corners
- Use wet rag to wash under all counters in kitchen into corners
- Garbage out

Mairead:
- Wash all kitchen chairs seat and backs by herself
- Use wet rag to wash under all counters in kitchen into corners
- Straighten shoes garage

Brighde
- Wash chairs
- Use wet rag to wash under all counters in kitchen into corners
- Be cute

Shealagh
- Wash chairs
- Use wet rag to wash under all counters in kitchen into corners
- Be cute

Emails Received After EWTN Appearance

I just delighted in watching and listening to you on EWTN Live this evening! Your gorgeous children and your "radical" "pouring out" of yourselves in your "YES" to God amount to some of the most inspiring faith I think I've ever seen. I was particularly moved by your profound grasp of the Faith and your easy, articulate expression of it throughout your interview. And what a rude shock it was to change the channel for a moment, after the close of your program with Fr. Mitch, and find myself instantly back in the secular, modern world of self-preoccupation. Thank you, thank you for your gracious, generous, love-filled witness! May God continue to bless you both, and all your children, with His ever deepening love and strength. *P.B.*

It was a great show. Ramona and I watched it from home in Hanceville. What a witness to the power and love of God and God's love for family life. *B.S.*

Dear Jim and Kathleen, After finishing your book I feel I actually do know you both plus your children. I liked the book very much and am recommending it to others. Gee, I feel like a piker with only 9 children. We wanted a dozen but after 7 miscarriages it was not to be. Kathleen, did you find that when women found out how many children you had (any over the number 5) the ladies would look at your face and then your stomach and then back to your face. It was something they all did!!!! Not sure what they were thinking but apparently they didn't see what they were looking for because they would then say, "You don't look like you had that many". The comments you wrote about I could identify with. We now have 22 grandchildren and 11 greats. God has blessed us abundantly. God bless each of you and carry on!!!! You are all doing a fine job. Know there are lots of challenges but lots of rewards, also. Keep the faith and keep smiling!!! Prayerfully yours, D.D. PS Much, much later. Interruptions. Are you familiar with them?????

Talk about a domestic church! Yours is like a cathedral! *S.S.*

Hi, I saw your interview with Fr. Mitch on EWTN and wanted to tell you how inspiring it was! I took my daughter to Mass this morning and it was great. We are going to try to go daily. *C.B.*

Very good presentation on EWTN. like to know what ages are your kids eldest to youngest. *L.R.*

I saw you on the live show this morning I would love to talk to you. God bless. *A.M.*

Saw you last night on EWTN and I ordered the DVD (1st time I ever did that). God bless your witness. *P.*

I just wonder how what your children answer to people and peers who may poke fun at or comment not too nicely on having so many siblings ... in this day and age of having only one or two children. I commend your family and will thank God there are Catholics like you, there to give example to the rest of us selfish Catholics, or so-called, right? Thank you. *H.P.*

Hi dear family! I am a Brazilian and I saw yesterday you program on EWTN. Was so beautiful and amazing grace for me to see and listen to you! I want to "thank you" from all my heart because I really think our families can and must go to Mass daily because the world is taking their peace... they don't know what it means to be a parent any more... and you gave me a lot of HOPE telling that YOU go to Mass! It´s not impossible! It´s God´s grace! May Our Lady keep giving you the grace to be this witness the world needs! *J.M., Brazil*

Hello, I accidentally stumbled upon the EWTN Live program today in which you and your wife were guests. I wanted to tell you 'thank you' for being what a true Catholic husband and father should be. You have become an example of what God created a Catholic man in the state of matrimony to be. You are a leader, a quality all but lost to men of the modern world, especially a spiritual leader, reminding me so much of Mr. Martin, Little Therese's father. I couldn't help crying watching you speak on EWTN with such joy of Faith, such gentleness yet power, such love for your wife and children, such strength in Faith..... It does my heart so much good to see that there ARE in the world happy families, happy marriages, Catholic lifestyle. How good it was to be reminded that good Catholic men like you exist. Thank you for being a ray of sunshine in a dark, lonely world. Thank you for being open and supportive of life. I rejoice seeing happiness, seeing the right way to live, seeing Catholicism in action. My heart REJOICES when I see happiness and Faith. Thank you for the encouragement. Thank you for your courage to live a Catholic lifestyle. Thank you and your wife for the sacrifices. Thank you for a wonderful example you are to the Mystical Body of Christ, to the world. *V.M.*

Dear Mr. & Mrs. Littleton, Am now watching you on EWTN. Thank you soooo much for your witness to bringing Christ's love into the world through your holy family. Thank you for your sacrifices for the Body of Christ. Thank you for your dedication to Our Lady of Guadalupe, Empress of the Americas and Mother of the Unborn. How awesome is our God and the work He is doing in you! May he continue to pour His blessings on you and yours as you do His Will, which is Love and Mercy itself. Prayerfully yours, *S.M.*

Hello Littleton Family, This morning we were so blessed to see your appearance on EWTN with Father Mitch. You are truly inspiring. *R.D.*

Hi Jim & Kathy, Thank so much for your witness about, your love for your 14 children, praise God that is just wonderful and I like your spiritual life with Jesus and Our Lady. *J.D.*

Hi James & Kathleen & Kids, My wife and I just happened to catch your interview tonight on EWTN Live with Fr. Mitch Pacwa. We greatly enjoyed listening to some of the experiences you have had and still have, whilst raising your family and felt a great affinity with you both. You see, we too are the parents of a largish Catholic family and hold very similar views on family life and parenting from what we could gather! Listening to your story was a comfort to us, as we like you live in an ever increasing secularized surrounding and are wading directly against the current. It is nice to know there are others making the same seemingly crazy choices elsewhere! You have a wonderful looking family and look to have a lot of fun and love in your home. We thought to send a quick note to say hi and promise to say a decade of the rosary for you all and also for your speaking tour. We certainly were inspired and wish you both all the best in this endeavour. *G.M., Australia*

Jim & Kathleen, We saw the show last night on EWTN. It was Great! Thank you for your witness to our Faith and for your friendship. We will keep the Littletons in our prayers. *P.A.*

Dear James and Kathleen, We were so happy to see you. Your beautiful family and your living faith on TV last night. Your life, your love and your faith is a great example to our Catholic faith. We thank God that such families do exist in our society today in this day and age. James, Kathleen we are so proud of you for raising so many children for your community. It just shows how unselfish you are. Let your children be a shining star and a guide for all the people around you. I too come from a large family. My mother and father had twelve children. My parents were very proud of us. I understand your family as we too had a very Catholic upbringing. I look back and I thank God for all those happy years we had together. Sadly my parents have gone to God and I miss them very much but we continue to carry the beautiful faith they gave us which no man can put a price to. We pray that you both will have a wonderful long and healthy life together for your children. As from my own experience I know that the most valuable gift and asset you can have in your life is your loving parents. May Our Blessed, kind, loving and compassionate Mother and Our Merciful Jesus grant you and your family all the Blessings that you deserve. May they keep you all under their loving protection always.
We thank you for coming alive on EWTN last night and for inspiring us.
Love and prayers. *J.T.*

Saw the show. Very impressive. I wish I could start over on my kids and follow their way of doing things, *C.F.*

Dear Kathleen and Jim, What a beautiful witness of your faithfulness To Jesus Christ, and all he has done in your lives!! What a wonderful testimony last night on TV!! We had to search the neighborhood to find someone who had EWTN, and after running to a couple of houses who all thought they had it, we finally found one that did!! It was perfect, as the house we watched it at, would have never watched something like that on TV, and I could tell throughout the show how they were just drawn in by what you had to say, and it had a powerful impact on them!!
Thank you for being such a gift to all of us!!! Your faith, Love, and charity, has touched us in so many ways, especially in our own walk with Christ. You have Inspired us to adopt these 3 new little ones coming our way, and we will always remember all the time, and support you have given us. Blessings upon you always, and thank you from the bottom of our hearts. *P.G.*

I just saw you on EWTN and was riveted to the television! Your story and ministry is amazing; keep up the good work!! We really appreciate hearing from families like yours; it is inspirational! *G.C.*

I am touched by your story. I come from a family of nine brothers and sisters. I enjoyed every moment. Love and God bless you abundantly always and may your story reach others. *L.G.*

Hello Littleton Family, This morning we were so blessed to see your appearance on EWTN with Father Mitch. You are truly inspiring. *R.D.*

James and Kathleen, I just saw you on the Christian station which I watch often. I don't remember the priest who interviewed you, but God Bless you and your children. I could have listened to both of you all night. Everything that was said just warmed my heart
I just delighted in watching and listening to you on EWTN Live this evening! *M.P.*

Dear Littletons, I just wanted to thank you for the wonderful program on EWTN this past week. We so much enjoyed listening to you both, what a great message of HOPE you all are for our world. When I saw you both on EWTN I called all of my friends and said you have to listen in to EWTN, there is this beautiful couple with 19 children, speaking so simply and so beautifully about family life! I do hope you will have the opportunity to be back some day on EWTN, you seemed so comfortable and natural before the cameras....

Also I think this is the "most powerful message for LIFE." *N.M.*

My wife and I are parents to 8 children. We watched you on EWTN Live last week. How blest are you and your family. It is inspiring to see other large families living out their Catholic faith. We enjoyed hearing about you on EWTN and plan to get a copy of your book in the near future. *P.C.*

Wisdom prevails! *M.K.*

About the Author

Kathleen Littleton is first and foremost, a wife and mother of nineteen children, fourteen living on earth and five in heaven. She is currently obtaining her Masters in Theological Studies from the Institute of Pastoral Theology of Ave Maria University while working as a Director of Religious Education at her home parish of St. Anthony's in Frankfort, Illinois and part-time for the Diocese of Joliet Tribunal. She obtained her Juris Doctorate Degree in Law from DePaul College of Law in Chicago, and a Bachelor of Science Degree in Secondary Education, English and French from the University of Illinois, Urbana. She gave up her career as an attorney to become a stay-at-home mother when her first child was born. With her husband of twenty-nine years, James Littleton, she co-authored *Better by the Dozen, Plus Two,* subtitled *Anecdotes and a Philosophy of Life from a Family of Sixteen* (2007), available at their website www.formingfaithfulfamilies.com, Amazon.com, and in bookstores. As Catholic reverts, spiritual guides, radio guests and contributors to Catholic.net, they are available as speakers or presenters, individually or as a couple, on a wide range of healing, marriage, and Faith and family topics. Their guest appearances on Catholic television and radio programs include: *EWTN Live* with Fr. Mitch Pacwa, November 11, 2009; EWTN's *Bookmark* with Doug Keck, May 9, 2010; *Light of the East*, host Fr Thomas Loya; *The Drew Mariani Show* on Relevant Radio; *Kresta in the Afternoon* on Ave Maria Radio; *The Doctor Is In* with Coleen Mast on Ave Maria Radio; and *Speak Now* with Susan Konig on Sirius Satellite Radio the Catholic Channel; and they have been featured in <u>Immaculate Heart Messenger</u> Magazine. Kathleen can be reached with questions, comments or speaking engagement requests at klittleped@aol.com or their website at www.formingfaithfulfamilies.com.

Endnotes:

[1] See Job 1:21.

[2] See *The Cloud of Unknowing* (Middle English: The Cloud of Unknowing) is an anonymous work of Christian mysticism written in Middle English in the latter half of the 14th century.

[3] See It's a Wonderful Life, an American Christmas drama film produced and directed by Frank Capra in 1947, that was based on the short story "The Greatest Gift", written by Philip Van Doren Stern.

[4] See The Wizard of Oz, a 1939 American musical fantasy film produced by Metro-Goldwyn-Mayer, directed primarily by Victor Fleming.

[5] See Appendix for more information on MomsMatter!

[6] See Appendix for various talks by the author that were published on Catholic.net and delivered at events and retreats over the years 2000-2011.

[7] See Appendix for Littleton Family Manual, referenced in Chapter One, page 14, *Better by the Dozen Plus Two,* by James and Kathleen Littleton, www.lulu.com publishing services, 2007.

[8] See James and Kathleen Littleton's website at www.formingfaithfulfamilies.com and the Appendix for links to and transcripts of some of these interviews.

[9] See James and Kathleen Littleton, *Better By the Dozen Plus Two,*(Lulu Publishing Services, 2007), chapter 3.

[10] St. Teresa (of Jesus) of Avila, *Exclamations of the Soul to God,* 15, 3.

[11] From Wikipedia: A General Confession, as understood by St. Ignatius of Loyola is a form of Confession whereby one spends three to ten days preparing for a confession of all one's sins in one's life up to that point in time. The main goal of the "general confession" is to turn one's life from one of sin to a more devout one(http://en.wikipedia.org/wiki/General_Confession).

[12] *Better by the Dozen Plus Two, Anecdotes and a Philosophy of Life from a Family of Sixteen,* James and Kathleen Littleton, Lulu Publishing Services, 2007 is available through www.lulu.com/littleton, Amazon, Barnes and Noble, and via the internet to purchase as a paperback or as an e-book.

[13] See James and Kathleen Littleton's website at www.formingfaithfulfamilies.com for audio link to their interviews on EWTN Live with Father Mitch Pacwa and Bookmark Show with Doug Keck (direct link: http://www.formingfaithfulfamilies.com/Speakers.html).

[14] See Appendix for an assortment of emails received after James and Kathleen Littleton's appearance on EWTN, November 2009.

[15] James M. Littleton, *Healed Through Cancer,* (Tate Publishing, 2012). See also: www.healedthroughcancer.com.
[16] Recounted in *Healed Through Cancer,* by James M. Littleton(Tate Publishing, 2012).